The Early English Settlement of Orkney and Shetland

The Early English Settlement of Orkney and Shetland

GRAEME DAVIS

First published in Great Britain in 2007 by
John Donald, an imprint of Birlinn Ltd

West Newington House
10 Newington Road
Edinburgh
EH9 1QS

www.birlinn.co.uk

ISBN 10: 0 85976 687 X
ISBN 13: 978 0 85976 687 6

British Library Cataloguing-in-Publication Data
A catalogue record for this book is available on request from the British Library

Typeset by Seán Costello

Printed and bound in Britain by Bell & Bain, Glasgow

Contents

Preface   ix

1   The Context   1

1.1 The Orkney and Shetland Environment   2

1.2 The Picts   6

1.3 In-comers   13

1.4 The Germanic Context   16

1.5 The Early English   23

1.6 The Vikings   29

1.7 The Scots   33

2   Historical Records   35

2.1 Diodorus Siculus   36

2.2 Claudius Claudianus   38

2.3   Pliny, Tacitus, Juvenal, Isidore   40

2.4   Nennius   42

2.5   The Anglo-Saxon Chronicle   45

2.6   Icelanders   47

2.7   Archaeology   48

2.8   Place-names   50

2.9   Genetics   53

2.10   History and the Early English   56

3   **Confirmation from Language**   58

3.1   Orkney and Shetland Norn   59

3.2   The Recorders of Orkney and Shetland Norn   67

3.3   Similarities with Old Norse and Old English   71

3.4   How Language Changes Work   75

3.5   *i*-Mutation in the Germanic Languages   78

3.6   The Absence of *i*-Mutation in Orkney and Shetland Norn   83

3.7   The Creation of Orkney and Shetland Norn   86

3.8   The Death of Orkney and Shetland Norn   89

4   **Texts in Orkney and Shetland Norn**   96

4.1   The Lord's Prayer   99

4.2   Sir Orfeo   100

4.3   The Cunningsburgh Phrase   101

4.4   George Low's Vocabulary   101

4.5   The Ballad of Hildina   102

4.6   Jakobsen's Foula Fragments   120

4.7   The Last Text in Orkney and Shetland Norn   120

4.8   Surviving Fragments   121

5   Impact   122

Sources   124

Bibliography   126

Index   128

Preface

BEFORE THE END of the Roman Empire, even before the English had begun their migration from Continental Europe to the land that would come to be called England, the English were to be found living in Orkney and Shetland.

Classical and mediaeval historians state that there was English presence in both Orkney and Shetland from at least the fourth century AD, therefore around a century before the English began their migration from the Continent to England. Their statements have been variously ignored, or dismissed as mistaken. They do not fit the familiar school-book view of an English migration from the Continent to England, starting around a century later in AD 449 with the landing of the brothers Hengist and Horsa in Kent.

This book looks again at the early settlements of the islands, and at the early historians' claims that the Early English were in Orkney and Shetland. It suggests that these statements are persuasive and should not be disregarded, but that in themselves they fall short of proof. Classical and mediaeval historians did make mistakes, and possibly their statements that the English were present in Orkney and Shetland are within this category of scholar error. Most writers about Orkney and Shetland today implicitly take this view, for they simply ignore the Early English presence in the islands.

New evidence presented in this book takes the story forward. An analysis of features in Orkney and Shetland Norn, the indigenous language of Orkney and Shetland which was spoken in the islands until the eighteenth century, serves as strong support for the accuracy of the assertions of early historians, for in its structures the language shows faint echoes of Anglo-Saxon, heavily overlaid by later Viking influences. Orkney and Shetland Norn is not merely a dialect of the Old Norse language with local modifications (as usually assumed), but rather a predominantly Old Norse language with certain embedded Anglo-Saxon features. It is therefore a language which emerged on the islands and is a unique – and neglected – part of the cultural heritage of Orkney and Shetland.

The Early English were a small group of settlers within the complex cultural mix of Orkney and Shetland, ultimately subsumed into the long-established indigenous population and the later Norwegian Viking population which migrated to the islands. The English did not survive as a discrete population, and were never more than a minority on the islands. Their impact on the islands is smaller than that of several other groups. Nevertheless, they had a four- or five-hundred-year presence in the islands, in its origin the earliest English settlement within the British Isles, and their settlement represents a surprising addition to the history of Orkney and Shetland. The language Orkney and Shetland Norn, while predominantly Old Norse in its vocabulary and grammatical structure, shows traces of the language spoken by these Early English, and these traces demonstrate that the English were present as settlers and not as mere visitors.

The concept of Orkney and Shetland Norn as an independent language, not merely a dialect of Old Norse, gives a new context for examining the surviving fragments of Orkney and Shetland Norn. The realisation that there is an Early English element in the cultural mix of the islands stresses the uniqueness of the literary achievement, which is not a mere off-shoot of Old Norse language and culture but an expression of a distinctive Orkney and Shetland culture.

In particular it stresses that the longest text in the language, *The Ballad of Hildina*, should be regarded as a literary monument within a language and culture unique to the islands.

1

The Context

THE EARLY ENGLISH settlement of Orkney and Shetland should be seen as one migration within the context of the settlement on the islands by several groups. The archaeology and early history of both Orkney and Shetland is particularly rich, providing evidence of the various migrations.

In ethnic terms as evidenced by DNA studies the two dominant strands in the migration patterns to both island groups are the first settlement by the Picts and the recent settlement by the Scots. The Picts have been the genetic and cultural bedrock through thousands of years. The Scots have been migrants in the last few centuries, and are a major genetic source. The islands are proud of their Viking heritage, which is a significant strand in the story of their settlement pattern and a feature more strongly evidenced in the islands than anywhere else in the British Isles. Yet compared with the impact of Picts and Scots, the Vikings are a secondary genetic and cultural influence. The Celts are also an influence on the islands, as are the various Christian missionary drives, mainly associated with the Celts. The Early English are a strand too, making a small and often overlooked contribution to the language, history, culture and ethnicity of Orkney and Shetland. They take their place as one of a parade of people who settled in the islands and who made their mark.

1.1 THE ORKNEY AND SHETLAND ENVIRONMENT

The Early English settlement described in this book occurred both in Orkney and Shetland, and the two island groups have therefore been treated together almost as if they are one unit. There are certainly similarities between the two island groups, and as Early English settlement occurred in both island groups it is appropriate within this book to treat them together. Yet the two groups are remarkable also for their differences, and it is noteworthy that Early English settlement occurred in two geographically and agriculturally dissimilar environments, and not in areas of the northern and eastern Scottish mainland, which in many respects resemble either Orkney or Shetland.

Orkney is predominantly low-lying with only moderate gradients, with the result that around a third of its land use today is arable. In earlier ages an even higher proportion would have been farmed, as non-mechanised agricultural techniques can cultivate gradients steeper than those which tractors can manage, as well as marginal plots at the edge of the sea. Today, as for many centuries, dairy farming is a major part of the economy of Orkney. Shetland by contrast is rugged, with steep gradients and little arable land. Today less than 4 per cent of the land area is farmed, and dairy farming uncommon. As in Orkney, earlier, less mechanised methods of farming would have enabled a higher proportion of the land to be farmed, but Shetland never supported anything approaching the arable acreage of Orkney. For settlers looking for land to farm it was Orkney that was the prize.

A requirement of all early farmers settling in the British Isles was that land had to be free of forest if it was to be viable, or at the most lightly wooded, as the work of felling a dense forest to clear a field for cultivation was so great as to be impractical. Until the modern era much of Scotland was forest, and therefore but sparsely settled, and most of what remained was undrained marshland or high moorland, therefore land of low agricultural value. Traditionally Scotland north of the Forth–Clyde valley, with the exception of the east-coast Mearns and some other locations close to the coast, had very little farm land. By contrast Orkney and Shetland were almost entirely without trees, and the light soils admirably suited to the tools available.

Both Orkney and Shetland offered food in abundance. The densely packed bird cliffs provide seabirds and their eggs from April to August, unlimited food available for the taking. The fishing grounds of the North Sea and North Atlantic were far richer than today, with fish available all year round. The natural fauna provided a high proportion of the food needs of the inhabitants. Farming – mainly sheep and corn, plus dairy on Orkney – satisfied other wants. Contrary to popular views of Orkney and Shetland as barren islands at the edge of the world, they were in fact some of the most food-rich for prehistoric and early historic peoples, and therefore some of the best places to live. The archaeology indicates that people were not spending the majority of their time in the finding and preparation of food, but rather had leisure time to build the remarkable monuments which so densely pack both island groups.

The seas between Orkney and Shetland are a substantial barrier. Even today the crossing, which is frequently rough because of the complex tides and surges, can be a difficult passage. Today people who live on the islands identify with one group or the other, and rarely or never visit the other group. The term 'The Northern Isles' exists more as an administrative convenience than as something that has meaning for the inhabitants. They are two separate entities.

Yet the position was different in late antiquity and through the Middle Ages. The ships that could transport people to either group and between islands could also transport people between the two groups. Rulers tended to rule both Orkney and Shetland. Indeed, in Viking times if an Earl of Orkney did not rule in Shetland also, he faced the likelihood of a rival raising a force there to attack him. Orkney was the richer land, but rule in Orkney alone was not safe. Orkney offered wealth: it was throughout the late Middle Ages and into the early modern period one of the richest of Scotland's counties by population size. Rule of Orkney was much prized, yet Orkney alone was not enough. It is Shetland that has the better geographic position. Voyaging to the east, Shetland is a straight run to Norway, a journey often helped by days of settled winds. The present ferry link from Lerwick to Bergen keeps alive a centuries-old tradition of close contact between Shetland and Norway. South from Shetland is a passage to the ports of the east coast of Scotland. Today Aberdeen has taken most of the shipping, though once Fraserburgh and Peterhead were important ports for Shetland. West is the route to Cape Wrath – the name means the cape of the turning point – and then south through the Sea of the Hebrides to Ireland. And north is the route to the Faroe Islands and on to Iceland – and in some past ages to Greenland and North America. Orkney offers agricultural bounty; Shetland offers geographical position as the crossroads of the North Atlantic. The two are a natural pairing for rulers and therefore for settlement.

The two island groups together have political strength. For most of history they should be regarded not as being at the edge of Britain, but as a North Atlantic crossroads. The Viking Earls of Orkney, ruling in both Orkney and Shetland, frequently expanded their influence south to Caithness and to Sutherland – the very name Sutherland meaning the south land, and south from the central perspective of Orkney. Often the influence of Orkney has pushed further south down the Scottish coast as far as the Cromarty Firth. At times the Faroe Islands have been under the sway of various Earls of Orkney. Rulers of Orkney and Shetland have held land in Iceland, and have been active in

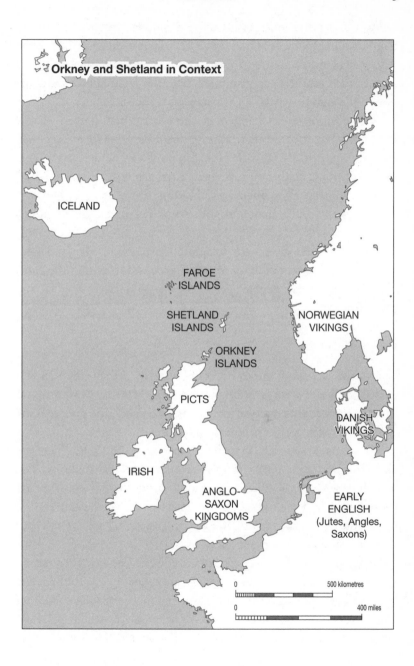

Orkney and Shetland in Context

ICELAND

FAROE
ISLANDS

SHETLAND
ISLANDS

ORKNEY
ISLANDS

NORWEGIAN
VIKINGS

PICTS

DANISH
VIKINGS

IRISH

ANGLO-
SAXON
KINGDOMS

EARLY
ENGLISH
(Jutes, Angles,
Saxons)

0   500 kilometres

0   400 miles

Norway and at the courts of Norwegian and Danish kings. There is a long-standing mercantile tradition which links Orkney and Shetland with the Hanseatic ports of the Baltic Sea, with Germany and the Netherlands, and with England. For centuries international trade has flowed through the ports of the two island groups.

The position is unchanged in the twenty-first century. Today Lerwick offers more destinations by direct passenger car ferry than any other port in the British Isles. Six ports can be reached (Aberdeen, Kirkwall, Hantsholm, Bergen, Torshavn and Seythisfjorthur) in five countries (UK, Denmark, Norway, Faroe Islands, Iceland). Today Shetland is re-emerging in its traditional role of the North Atlantic crossroads.

As befits their crossroads location, Orkney and Shetland have been home to a great number of ethnic groups. It is within the complex ebb and flow of people and cultures that the Early English find their place.

1.2 THE PICTS

One of the earliest groups to reach the islands – perhaps the very first – was the Picts. For all practical purposes the Picts may be regarded as the indigenous inhabitants of Orkney and Shetland, and are the starting point for a survey of peoples and cultures.

Much information is available to us about the Picts. There are extensive and frequently impressive archaeological remains. The Romans speak of the Picts. The people survived well into the historic period, and are the group who united with the Scots to create the medieval kingdom of Scotland. Yet everything we know about the Picts simply raises more questions.

The name Pict comes from Roman commentators, and is related to the Latin verb 'to paint'. The Picts are called by the Romans the painted or tattooed people, though the name is puzzling as neither archaeology nor historic sources have been able to support the use either of body paint or tattoos. What the people called themselves we do not know. At the time of the Roman Empire the Picts were found in the British Isles north of the Forth–Clyde valley, therefore the whole of the present Highlands plus Fife and Angus, and including Orkney and Shetland and the Western Isles. There was also a group of Picts south of the Clyde in what is today Galloway. One of the southern tribes of Picts was called by the Romans the Caledonii – possibly reflecting the name the people themselves used – and Caledonia has become an alternative name for Scotland, reflecting the Pictish heritage of the whole of Scotland.

It is most likely that we should understand Pictish culture in terms of two distinct phases – though even this broad distinction is not universally accepted. There is an early pre-Celtic phase, which existed from prehistoric times until possibly AD 100 – there is no consensus on dating. It is believed that these people were of a non-Indo-European ethnicity, spoke a non-Indo-European language, and had a religion, culture and social structure distinct from other peoples of the British Isles. It has been suggested that their language may have been related to the one modern long-established non-Indo-European language in Europe – Basque – though there seems at present no way to test this intriguing idea. The subsequent phase of Pictish culture is characterised by Picts who have adopted a Celtic culture and who are speaking a Celtic language. Presumably we must envisage a migration of Celtic speakers into the Pictish area bringing in a new language and culture, and presumably around AD 100, though the date is far from settled.

The Picts have left two enduring puzzles, both well exemplified in Orkney and Shetland: their writing and their brochs.

Pictish writing uses a script called Ogham, which was used also for the early Irish language, though whether invented by the Picts or the Irish is not known. The script is an alphabet, at first sight dissimilar from the alphabets with which we are familiar today, but utilising the familiar European principle of a limited set of symbols representing both vowels and consonants. Both Latin and Runic alphabets have been suggested as possible sources for Ogham, though neither is an obvious source. What is remarkable is that a new alphabet was invented rather than an existing one being adopted, a state of affairs which seems to indicate a sophisticated culture, as well as a specific need. Possibly this need is as simple as a requirement for an alphabet that could easily be carved on stone, and there is no doubt that Ogham's straight lines suitable for notching the edge of a stone are particularly suited to this purposes. Most Ogham inscriptions are in a Celtic language, effectively Old Irish. Probably some Ogham texts are in another earlier language, presumably reflecting the pre-Celtic language spoken by the earlier Picts. Sadly, so few texts survive in Ogham script in any language that we have substantial problems of decipherment, particularly with those from Orkney and Shetland. All are stone inscriptions which are badly weathered, and all are very short. There is a working assumption that many of them are grave markers, and that the inscription is likely to be the name of the deceased. Some scholars believe they can distinguish the form name + mac + name, therefore a Celtic language patronymic, though even this cautious and basic translation is not uniformly accepted. We are in the frustrating position of having a literate ancient people who have left us texts in their own alphabet, but texts which we are largely unable to read. Yet that some of the early inhabitants of Orkney and Shetland were literate, and perhaps even inventors of an alphabet, is in itself reason to accept the early inhabitants as a people with a high level of culture.

A second outstanding achievement of the Picts is the building of the structures called brochs. A broch is a round, dry-stone building, with walls in the region of 10 feet thick, and an internal diameter of from 17 feet to 50 feet, with a height of up to 40 feet. These measurements describe stone age buildings which are massive structures and would have taken much time and labour to build, indicating a construction programme which required organisation of very large labour forces. There are over 500 of these structures known in Scotland, including well over 100 in each of Orkney and Shetland. They are found only in the Pictish area, though curiously there are Pictish areas in which brochs were not built. Quite how this distribution might be resolved remains a puzzle. There have been suggestions that they must have been built by a people other than the Picts to account for the distribution, though there seems to be little evidence to support such a view, and the general consensus is that they are Pictish. Certainly within Orkney and Shetland it is very hard to see who else could have built them.

Dating the brochs is far from easy, though broad parameters have been established. For example, the best preserved, the Broch of Mousa in Shetland, belongs to the broad period 100 BC–AD 100. Many appear to be somewhat earlier, and around AD 100 seems to be the terminus for broch building. From the date it appears that the brochs belong to the culture of the pre-Celtic Picts.

Brochs are the biggest and most sophisticated examples of dry-stone walling ever produced. Their outer walls are galleried, which means that there was an inner and outer wall tied together for strength, with a cavity between which could accommodate a staircase. The structures had a waist, and an overall shape that to the modern eye resembles a power station cooling tower, a simple elegance of design which may perhaps have been intentional. The double wall is breached by just one doorway, which is so low as to be virtually a crawl-way, and which could be closed from the inside by a large stone. The usual view today is that the brochs were probably roofed with thatch on a wooden frame, though this is far from proved, and in view of the hundreds of brochs known it is surprising that not one has produced any definite evidence of a roof. On the contrary, in Orkney and Shetland, where there were no large trees, the origin of the timber that could provide structural beams to roof a 50-foot void is a puzzle. In all brochs the top stone courses have been lost to the ravages of time, so we have no direct evidence one way or the other for the seatings for roof beams.

The biggest puzzle is that we have no certainty on what the function of the brochs might have been. There is no shortage of ideas, but none that are convincing. Most writers state that they were defensive, and it is true that they would have been all but impossible to break into. However the explanation of a defensive structure simply does not stand up to scrutiny. First of all, there is no obvious enemy, and civil disturbance seems an unlikely justification for such a massive structure. The enclosed area is relatively small, certainly disproportionately small with respect to the labour that went into the surrounding wall. Very few brochs have a well, so they could not have withstood a siege. Nor do they have an adequate area for rainwater catchment, even in the rainy climate of Orkney and Shetland. The entrance is so small that cattle, pigs and horses could not have been brought in, while sheep and goats could have been brought in only with great difficulty, and certainly not quickly. These were not suitable structures to safeguard livestock. Nor do they seem designed for the storage of grain or any other commodity. The height is excessive for defence – most classical and medieval fortifications had far lower walls – while offensive action was largely precluded by the waisted shape and the height. Furthermore, the brochs are rarely built on defensive sites, where the landscape would have assisted a defensive role. While it is possible that the brochs were at times pressed into service as makeshift defensive buildings, this cannot have been their primary function. Brochs were not castles. Nor were they look-out towers, as they are rarely sited in an area where there is a particular view. A novel idea is that they were status symbols declaring the power of a local ruler, almost the stately homes of their day, and that their height and size were intended to impress by reaching the maximum that can be achieved with a dry-stone-walling technology. Perhaps this is so, but there is almost nothing to support this idea. Instead, to the contrary, it may be noted that most brochs are in sight of at least one other broch, which argues against their being the home of a local noble controlling a significant local area. Recently the idea has come to the fore that brochs are neither castles nor stately homes, but contained within them the industries of a village settlement – that they were the factories and markets of the day, perhaps with multiple floors within them. It is hard to dismiss absolutely such an idea, but the evidence to support it is very thin indeed. Brochs, like Ogham, remain a Pictish mystery.

The first phase of Pictish culture was witnessed by the Romans. In the year AD 82 (or possibly 83) the Roman general Agricola with a fleet of galleys circumnavigated the British Isles and visited Orkney, though we have been given no description of the Romans' impressions of Orkney. The Romans had by this time subdued most of Britain, and were pushing north into the Pictish lands. In AD 83 a major battle was fought between the Romans and the Picts. The location is given in Roman sources as Mons Graupius, not certainly identified today, but generally considered to be within modern Aberdeenshire. The Roman force is variously estimated at 15,000 and 20,000 soldiers – an immense army for the age – and they were confronted by a much larger Pictish army, which Roman sources state was 30,000 men. Maybe there is some exaggeration in these figures (in particular the Romans liked to claim that they were outnumbered in battles) but we do have the impression of a very large battle. At Mons Graupius the Romans had the victory through better tactics and iron discipline. They reported 10,000 Picts killed.

The battle is recorded in some detail by Tacitus, including an account of the speech given by the Pictish general to his confederacy of troops. The record of the speech in some respects stretches credulity (how did the Romans learn of a speech given by the enemy? Who translated it?) yet Tacitus is a respected source and at the very least the speech seems to express what the Romans thought were Pictish values. If we are to believe it as genuine we have just about the only recorded utterance by the Picts, and therefore a text which may give us a glimpse of the cultural and ethical values of the Pictish society of Orkney and Shetland:

> When I consider the origin of this war and the necessities of our position, I have a sure confidence that today this union of yours will be the beginning of freedom to the whole of Britain. Slavery is unknown to all of us. We, the most renowned nation in Britain,

dwelling in the very heart of the country, out of sight of the shores of the conquered, have even kept our eyes unpolluted by the defilement of slavery. We are the last people on earth and the last to be free. Our very remoteness in a land known only by rumour has protected us up till this day. But now there is no people beyond us, nothing but tides and rocks and, more deadly than these, the Romans, from whose oppression escape is vainly sought by obedience and submission. Our goods and fortunes they would collect for their tribute, our harvests for their granaries. They plunder, they butcher, they rape. Which will you choose, to follow me into battle, or to submit to taxation, labour in the mines and all the other tribulations of slavery? Whether you are to endure these forever or take a quick revenge, this battle must decide. Since then you cannot hope for quarter, take courage. Let us, then, a fresh and unconquered people, never likely to abuse our freedom, show forthwith at the very first onset what heroes Caledonia has in reserve. Rome is held together by success and will be broken up by disaster. (*The Germany and Agricola of Tacitus*, trans. Edward Brooks, Oxford, 1897)

While Mons Graupius was a defeat for the Picts, the Romans were unable to follow up their victory and were driven from the north of the country. Indeed, the Romans suffered horrific losses in a series of smaller battles before retreating. Despite a further two invasions, the Romans never conquered the Picts, instead creating and defending a northern frontier through the building of Hadrian's Wall and the Antonine Wall. The land of the Picts, and that part of Pictland that was Orkney and Shetland, stayed beyond Roman rule and largely beyond Roman knowledge.

At Mons Graupius and in other early encounters with the Romans under Agricola, the Picts suffered great losses. Presumably this created disruption within their society. Although the Roman attackers were ultimately defeated, the impact of invasion may well have been the loss of the early phase in Pictish culture. We know that the building of brochs came to an abrupt end around AD 100. It is plausible that this is the date when the Celts arrived, and the second

Celtic phase of Pictish society began. Possibly, therefore, the Celtic arrival is linked with the disruptions caused by the Roman attacks.

The Picts of this second phase in Orkney and Shetland and elsewhere in many respects resemble Celtic Ireland. Their material culture is comparable, and they had an artistic style which closely resembles that of Ireland. They soon followed the Irish as early converts to Christianity. The linguistic change to speaking a Celtic language, essentially Old Irish, demonstrates the extent of cultural ascendancy of the Celts throughout the Pictish lands. Such a change suggests a Celtic ruling class, maintaining their dominance for generations, and imposing their language. From around AD 100 Orkney and Shetland were culturally Celtic. However, the Celtic incomers were not numerous, and in ethnic terms the people of Orkney and Shetland remained essentially Pictish, as they do to this day. The impact of later migrations: Celts, Early English, Vikings, Scots, has diluted the original Pictish ethnicity, but it remains the dominant element.

1.3 In-Comers

In the fourth and fifth centuries AD Orkney and Shetland were visited by several groups who had a lasting impact on the islands. One of these groups, from about the early fourth century, was the Early English, but more about these later.

Other groups of in-comers were associated with Christian missionary activity. The Christian faith arrived in Orkney and Shetland through two waves of missionary activity, accompanied by small-scale migration of peoples into the islands.

St Ninian is the missionary to the Picts and one of the in-comers to Orkney and Shetland. In his long life – more than seventy years from around AD 358 to 432 – he brought Christianity to an enormous area of the north of Britain. From his home in the vicinity of the Solway Firth in what was the old Celtic kingdom of Rheged he travelled to Rome, where he was both made a bishop by Pope

Siricius and given the task of evangelising the Picts. Back in Britain he established his base at Whithorn on the north shore of the Solway Firth, today Wigtownshire, still within the Celtic kingdom of Rheged but close to the southernmost Pictish kingdom. He called his church there by the Latin name 'Candida Casa', meaning 'White House', and from there he preached the gospel of (in his words) the 'White Christ'. St Ninian's missionary activities on the east coast of Scotland and to both Orkney and Shetland are at the borderline between history and myth, yet whatever the truth of his exploits his memory remains. In Orkney and Shetland churches dedicated to him abound: at opposite ends of Orkney both North Ronaldsay and South Ronaldsay have chapels to St Ninian, while in Shetland there is a St Ninian's on Yell; but most impressive are the chapel and well dedicated to him on Shetland's St Ninian's Isle; all these are testament to the early missionary zeal which brought Christianity at such an early date to the northernmost extremity of the British Isles. Thanks to St Ninian, Christianity had at least a toehold in Orkney and Shetland from the early fifth century.

The second wave of missionary activity is an outreach from the Iona community of St Columba, itself a mission of Celtic Christianity from the early Irish Church. Perhaps we should understand from this second conversion that St Ninian's missionary work in Orkney and Shetland had been incomplete. Perhaps there is an explanation in terms of language. While St Ninian spoke a language akin to Welsh, St Columba and his followers spoke Irish Gaelic, much closer to the Celtic speech of the later Picts in Orkney and Shetland. St Ninian brought a foreign language and new religion; St Columba brought an already part-established religion and preached it in the peoples' own language. St Columba brought Irish Christianity from Iona to all the Picts of the north of Britain. As much a warrior as a saint, he used Iona as a staging post for missionary activity into Pictland. History or myth – the boundaries are blurred – tell that he travelled north-east from Iona through the length of the Great Glen, famously encountering the Loch Ness monster, which he pacified with a blessing. At Inverness at the court of the Pictish King Bridei I, Iona Christianity took root, and spread from there to the lands which owed allegiance to King Bridei. Included within these was the Kingdom of Orkney, a minor Pictish kingdom – and presumably including Shetland within the title of Orkney.

By the end of the sixth century Christianity was established in Orkney and Shetland, seemingly as the dominant religion. The islands had joined the international cultural community that was the Christian church, and which made possible movement of people and ideas throughout Christendom. As Iona was the mother church to which Christianity in Orkney and Shetland looked for governance, links with Iona were crucial. So too were links with other churches founded from Iona. On Scotland's east coast in the Firth of Forth is Inchcolm, the island of St Columba, which served as an Iona-in-the-East. Visited by St Columba in AD 567 and founded then or shortly after, the Inchcolm church was more accessible from Orkney and Shetland than Iona – it is both shorter in miles and a less exposed route than sailing to Iona round Cape Wrath.

Missionary activity from Iona led through Inchcolm to Lindisfarne on the Northumbrian coast, which like Iona and Inchcolm is an island community. The nature of this community gives an idea of how the multicultural mix of Orkney and Shetland may have functioned. The traditional date of foundation of the Lindisfarne church is around AD 635, therefore just a little after Christianity was consolidated in Orkney and Shetland. Because of the subsequent literary output of Northumbria, particularly the *Ecclesiastical History* and *Life of St Aidan*, both by Bede, something is known about the early community in Lindisfarne. In particular, it was international in character. St Aidan himself was an Irishman, Connaught born, who had spent time in Iona, and arrived in Northumbria as head of a Gaelic-speaking Christian mission. The King of Northumbria, Oswald, was another international figure. He had travelled to Iona in his youth, and learned Gaelic there. Indeed, there is a story that the king himself translated the preaching of St Aidan. Lindisfarne welcomed scholars and pilgrims from far and wide, and was linguistically and culturally rich. The language of Northumbria was English, but the proximity of the Celtic lands west of the Pennines ensured that there were many Welsh speakers there. The Northumbrian poet Caedmon, remembered today as the first poet in English, bears a Welsh name and presumably springs from a Welsh culture. The Church brought Gaelic from Ireland and Iona. It brought Latin too, so that from its inception there were men on Lindisfarne who spoke and wrote in the language of the Roman Church. Probably there were Greek-speakers too, as a few Greek words are preserved in written texts. Lindisfarne was an international community – and so in their way were the communities of Orkney and Shetland. Within their multi-ethnic mix they accommodated groups who were not from the indigenous Pictish ethnicity, groups which included the Early English.

1.4 THE GERMANIC CONTEXT

The migration which brought the Early English to Orkney and Shetland is part of a Europe-wide movement of peoples, and must be understood in this wider context.

Around the time of Christ a people called by the Romans 'Germanic' were living in much of northern Europe. Their lands correspond roughly with that of modern Germany, plus the Low Countries and Austria, plus southern Scandinavia. In ethnic, cultural and linguistic terms these people are the ancestors of today's Germanic peoples, including the English, the Germans and Austrians, the Dutch and the Scandinavians.

Quite how long the Germanic peoples had been living in this territory is not clear from either historical or archaeological sources. It was once held that this territory was their homeland, or that at least they had been there for many centuries. Today the view has shifted to see the Germanic peoples as migrants who came from somewhere to the east – perhaps the Russian steppes – and who settled in these lands shortly before the birth of Christ. Presumably their arrival would have displaced an earlier indigenous people, though at this we can only guess. Early on there seems to have been a split between the Continental Germanic population, and the population living to the north in Scandinavia. In linguistic terms this is represented by the West Germanic languages of English, German and Dutch, and the North Germanic languages, the languages of Scandinavia. This view gains unexpected support from the Icelandic medieval historian Snorri Sturluson, who in *Heimskringla* tells what is generally regarded as a foundation myth of the Germanic peoples, describing a migration into northern Europe from the east, and a split into two ruling dynasties, one on the Continent and one in Scandinavia.

The early Germanic peoples cannot be regarded as illiterate as they had their own alphabet – runic – from perhaps as early as the third century AD. However, early texts in Germanic written in the runic script consist of little more than the name of an individual commemorated on a memorial stone, and provide almost no information about the people. The early Germanic peoples were literate, but they were not great writers. For written sources we look to Rome, and have an account of the Germanic peoples written by the Roman historian Tacitus, yet one which we must treat with care. His presentation of the Germanics is flattering in the extreme, for Tacitus wished to contrast the society and government of the Germanic peoples with what he saw as a corrupt and indolent Roman society in his age. In effect he was writing a political pamphlet and not an objective description. He presents a picture of noble and heroic Germanics, living in well-governed societies, and with qualities both moral and physical lacking among the Romans. The account is of course propaganda, though like all effective propaganda it contained much within it that was true. It may be noted, for example, that the Romans had suffered several crushing defeats at the hands of the Germanic people, suggesting that they possessed governmental structures able to raise mass armies and deploy them against the Roman legions. Archaeology of the Germanics shows a material culture that makes extensive use of the available natural resource of the area – wood – which, of course, rarely survives, so we are without the grand archaeological sites of the type which have been preserved in the Mediterranean basin and the Near East. Yet enough has survived to show a high degree of civilisation.

Tacitus gives the very first written mention of the Early English people, described as Angles (English), Jutes and Saxons. Living around the Rhine estuary, the Angles are grouped with two other kindred peoples, the Jutes and the Saxons. Tacitus states that they worshipped an earth-mother goddess called Ing, and so the three groups may be called Ingvaeonic. He also delivers the humbling first historical description of the English people, stating that they are 'of little note'.

The linking of three peoples – the English or Angles, the Saxons and the Jutes – is relevant through late antiquity and the early Middle Ages. That there were three distinct groups with three adjacent home territories is in little doubt, but it has little subsequent significance as their development was as one people. The three groups had the same language and culture, were all interrelated, and for all practical purposes Jute, Angle and Saxon may all be regarded as synonyms for English. The Romans certainly thought of them as one, and even today a speaker of Lowland Scots might refer to an English person not as an Angle but as a Sassenach, a Saxon.

It is in the fourth century that the English people began to have an impact on the Roman Empire. The boundary between Rome and the Germanic world was one of the less well defined and more fluid at the edge of the Roman Empire – there was no Hadrian's Wall here – but by the third century a land frontier had been established. More of a problem to Rome was the sea frontier, for the Germanics became good seafarers. The Germanic peoples must have used boats even before contact with the Romans, for they had spread from the Danish peninsula across the sea to what is now Sweden and Norway.

However, these boats were rudimentary. The ships which the Germanics came to use were copied from Roman models as a consequence of contact with Rome.

The maintenance of Britain as an integral part of the Roman Empire required continuous sea-borne traffic across what is now the English Channel, and for this the Romans used ships that were as advanced as any then in use. They built ships with an inner frame onto which the external planking was nailed, creating a robust and seaworthy vessel, but one which was heavy, slow and cumbersome. These ships were certainly adequate for crossing the English Channel and indeed for voyaging much further, but they had very limited capacity to move in any direction other than that in which the wind was blowing. They could not tack, and rowing in the open sea was rarely practical due to their great weight – indeed, rowing was mainly used for precise manoeuvres over short distances within harbours or other sheltered waters. This key directional limitation accompanied by rudimentary navigational skills encouraged the sort of voyaging that may be characterised as waiting for a settled wind in the required direction, and making a short hop to the next port while the wind lasts. It also discouraged voyaging out of sight of land. In the island-strewn Mediterranean this was rarely a problem, and the English Channel could be crossed without violating this principle, for in Roman times with clear air much of the English Channel was narrow enough to see across. Even today with the ubiquitous pollution reducing visibility, it is still sometimes possible to see across the English Channel with the naked eye.

The English borrowed their ship design from the Romans. The result was that they could go wherever the Romans went, and as the Romans had no effective navy they could go without restriction. Indeed, so common did English incursions become on the south-east coasts of Roman Britain that the Romans created a robust series of defences to protect what they called the 'Saxon Shore'. These fortifications functioned less to keep the Saxons out than to regulate contact with them, so that their raiding became trading. Extensive trade between Romans and English took place, with the 'Saxon Shore' becoming a regulated market. A settled colony of English merchants was even established in Roman Britain on the Thames just down-river from their capital of London at what is today Hackney.

The Early English were a force to be reckoned with. The North Sea itself was called by the Romans the 'Germanic Ocean', reflecting the dominance of the English and other Germanic peoples in these waters – and implying that Roman rule did not run in this sea. Early English traders worked throughout the North Sea, but along coastal routes rather than directly across the sea. Essentially there were two routes. These were on the east side of the Germanic Ocean, from the Rhine estuary along the coasts of Denmark and Norway, and on the west side from the Rhine estuary to the 'Saxon Shore' and further along the coast of south-east Britain both west and north. Trade direct across the North Sea was presumably minimal, reflecting the preference for voyages in sight of land.

It is this English expansion through the Germanic Ocean which ultimately brought the Early English to Orkney and Shetland. The Roman shore defences against the Saxons were formalised only in the south-east, but Saxon incursions and Roman defence against them doubtless occurred beyond this margin. The English had ac-cess to the full length of the east coast of Roman Britain as far as the River Tyne at the eastern end of Hadrian's Wall. North of this in what we now call Scotland, the English would have found little to interest them. The Picts inhabiting most of this area were not as rich as the Roman Britons for trade purposes, and anyway had little that the English wanted. For hundreds of miles the east coast both of Roman Britain and of Scotland was covered in forest, the now-lost Great Caledonian Forest, with very few areas free from trees. For farmers with the basic tools available to the English, such land was not suitable for cultivation. The effort needed to fell and remove the root of even one full-grown tree is formidable, and to clear enough land to create fields for farming is simply not practical. Settlement would not have been attempted. Only in the far north of Scotland,

and in Orkney and Shetland was unforested land found, which the Early English would have been able to farm. It would have been strange indeed had they not coveted this land.

The seaward advance of the Germanic people certainly concerned the Roman Empire, but the more alarming threat to Rome was the advances made by the Germanics in the south and east. Within a couple of generations a series of mass migrations of Germanics took place in numbers so great that they swamped the Roman Empire and brought about its end. It is difficult to find a modern parallel. This was a Germanic mass exodus from the east and north of Europe in search of prosperity within the boundaries of the Roman Empire, where whole families with their belongings and livestock marched alongside vast armies, forming hordes which travelled for years before settling, a whole nation living for generations from the plunder of the lands they passed through.

In the 370s one of the largest eastern Germanic people, the Visigoths, crossed into the Roman Empire and settled in great numbers in Roman Moesia, today's Bulgaria. Having started to move, they became a semi-nomadic people, a state of affairs which made it very hard for them to settle. At the battle of Adrianople in AD 378 they defeated the Eastern Roman Emperor, Valens, and marched into Rumelia and Macedonia. By AD 395 they had reached Greece, and for a time it looked as if they would settle there. Yet from AD 399 the movement continued, this time north along the Dalmatian coast, and subsequently into the Italian peninsula. In AD 410 they made their attack on Rome, and following their victory they sacked the city. To future historians, AD 410 was the end of the Roman Empire. Yet the Visigoths were not finished. After travelling the length of Italy, the Visigoths turned and retraced their steps to northern Italy, then turned west, arriving in AD 507 in what is now central Spain, where they created a Visigothic kingdom of Iberia. The Goths ruled Spain for more than two centuries.

The Visigoths were not alone. Their Germanic cousins the Ostrogoths made their own migration through the Balkans and

into northern Italy in the 450s. West across the Rhine whole nations of Germanic peoples poured into Roman Gaul, creating the
Frankish and Burgundian kingdoms. The Lombards, close relatives
of the Early English, crossed the Alps and established a Lombard
kingdom in northern Italy. Nor were the Germanics the only people to take part in these mass migrations, for very many other peoples were caught up in these movements. For example, the Visigoth
hordes came to include many Diaspora Jews who had been living
in Greece, carrying them with them as far as Spain, with the consequence that in Spain in the Middle Ages the names Goth and
Jew are used as virtual synonyms. Also moving into western Europe
were the Vandals. Though not a Germanic people (the Vandals came
from somewhere east of the Ukraine), they passed through the heart
of the Germanic lands and caught up many Germanics with them,
so when they crossed the Rhine into Roman Gaul they were a mixed
group. Their migration is one of the longest, taking them through
Gaul and Spain, across the Straits of Gibraltar, east along the north
African coast to Carthage, then by sea to Rome, sacked for a second time in AD 455. Their action gave Europe the concept and word
'vandalism'.

The Roman province of Britain escaped these incursions. In
AD 410 during the months before Rome fell, the Roman governor
of Britain sent a letter to Rome asking for reinforcements. His letter
has been preserved in Rome, along with the transcript of the reply,
which stated that Britain must 'look to her own defences'. However
great the problems were in Britain at this time, some form of Roman
order did continue even after the fall of Rome, and the Saxon shore
defences remained in place. It was to be another forty years before
the English began their incursions into Britain.

The fall of the Roman Empire as a consequence of Germanic
migrations illustrates the massive scale of these incursions. While
the Germanics certainly won battles, the overwhelming cause of
their success was their sheer numbers. The concept is useful in
understanding the English attacks on Roman Britain. While each

individual ship contained just a very small band of men, the ships were coming in very great numbers. Indeed, their numbers are hinted at by the massive fortifications the Romans built along the Saxon Shore to keep them out. In the context of a North Sea crossed by large numbers of Germanics over a long time period, there is no surprise that some English reached as far as the north of that sea – Orkney and Shetland. Indeed, it would be strange if they had not.

1.5 THE EARLY ENGLISH

The Early English are the overlooked group in the history of Orkney and Shetland. There is no clear first date for their visits to the islands, or for their first settlement. The historical records discussed below place them there from the second half of the fourth century AD, while the linguistic evidence, again discussed below, must have the Early English in the islands before around AD 400. A reasonable estimate of their arrival is in the first half of the fourth century AD. This corresponds with the increasing incursions of the Early English on the Saxon Shore of Roman Britain, and is therefore a likely date. It cannot be much later, and while an earlier date would fit the linguistic evidence it seems implausible.

Incursions by the Early English on the coast of Roman Britain begin around AD 280. The Roman response culminated in the creation of nine forts on the south and east coast of Britain as key defences against what they called the Saxon threat. The forts range from Portchester Castle in Hampshire, along the south coast and up the east coast as far as Brancaster in Norfolk. The nine as recorded in *Notitia Dignitatum* are: Portchester Castle, Pevensey, Lympne, Dover, Richborough, Reculver, Bradwell-on-Sea, Burgh Castle and Brancaster, and together they represent a massive building operation. Defence of the Saxon Shore was entrusted by the Romans to a high-ranking official with the title *comes litoris Saxonici*, Count of the Saxon Shore. The scale of the Romans' defensive effort is an indication of the enormous size of the threat. The great Roman Empire was facing not an occasional incursion by a stray Saxon ship, but rather sustained attack continued over many decades. At times the Saxon threat was controlled by organised trade, and a function of the forts of the Saxon Shore was trading posts. Yet the threat of attack was never far away, and often broke out into warfare. In AD 367, for example, the Early English along with other British allies including the Picts posed a serious military threat to Roman Britain, and killed the then Count of the Saxon Shore, one Nectaridus.

For seafarers who could cross the North Sea to the south-east of Britain, further voyaging along the coasts of Britain was practical. When it suited the Early English to trade, they could sail for one of the forts on the Saxon Shore, or to an English trading post on the Thames just down-river from Roman London. When they wished plunder, sailing beyond the defences of the Saxon Shore was straightforward. West of Portchester the Early English frequently made incursions against Roman Britain. Similarly they were a constant threat north of Brancaster. In the north of the Roman province of Britain an innovative solution was found, in that Saxons were pressed into service as mercenaries fighting on Hadrian's Wall defending the northern boundary of the Roman Empire. Further north we simply do not have the records. It is inconceivable that the ships that attacked Roman Britain in such numbers did not voyage further north, to the Pictish kingdoms. Indeed the frequent co-ordination of Saxon and Pictish attacks on Roman Britain demonstrates the extent of contact, and hints that the Picts and Saxons came to some sort of accommodation. Roman accounts and the accounts of early post-Roman historians place the Early English in Orkney and Shetland. The Early English voyaged as far as it was possible to go, travelling from their Continental home to the far north of Britain by a serious of steps never out of sight of land.

The Early English therefore arrive in Orkney and Shetland shortly before St Ninian, and take their place in a multi-ethnic mix.

Around AD 410 – the year when the Roman Empire fell – the ethnic and language mix of Orkney and Shetland was as follows:

1. The Non-Indo-European Picts. These must have been the dominant ethnicity, as even today this group is the primary genetic heritage of the islands. Possibly some spoke their original non-Indo-European language, though a Celtic language had been spoken on the islands for over three centuries.
2. The Celts. A numerically small group who had brought their language and culture to Orkney and Shetland. They were speaking a Celtic language in the Gaelic sub-group, basically Old Irish, and this language had been adopted by most, perhaps all, of the Picts. Gaelic, or Old Irish, was the dominant language of the islands.
3. The Early English. Again a numerically small group, but with their own Germanic language. This group would have communicated easily with all Germanic visitors, including the ancestors of the Vikings who crossed from Norway, and would have perceived themselves as ethnically one with all the Germanic peoples.
4. The Christian missionaries of the St Ninian mission. Their mother tongue was what linguists term a P-Celtic language, the sub-group which is represented today by Welsh and Breton. Their language was essentially Welsh, and though related to the Gaelic spoken on the islands not mutually comprehensible with it. Presumably they learned Gaelic to carry out their apostolic mission. And surely they, like St Ninian, knew Latin.

Such was the multiculturalism of Orkney and Shetland. Three, perhaps four, languages were spoken on the islands, and four ethnic groups were represented. This environment appears to have existed on both groups of islands, so that all three or four languages and all four ethnicities were represented from Unst in Shetland to South Ronaldsay in Orkney.

Such a situation is paralleled today in many communities. Cities around the world have communities speaking a variety of languages, and maintaining them for generations. Europe has the specific examples of the Jewish and Gypsy populations maintaining their culture and language for centuries, even millennia, although vastly outnumbered by host populations. The former USSR and the USA are full of instances of villages or small towns which preserve a language and culture brought by a migrant group. The situation which existed in Orkney and Shetland is reasonably commonplace as a cultural and language environment.

The Christian missionaries provided a link with the south, with the culture and scholarship of Roman Britain and the Roman Empire. Their Welsh and Latin were languages of scholarship and we may guess of writing, though nothing from Orkney and Shetland has been preserved. The majority of the population spoke Gaelic, and if any of the original non-Indo-European Pictish language survived it was fast dying. Gaelic was the predominant language, and Pictish the ethnicity and culture, though the brochs of the earlier Pictish phase were now disused for over three hundred years and beginning to fall into disrepair. The Early English were living alongside the Picts, though quite what their respective roles were is not clear.

This ethnic, cultural and linguistic environment was scarcely modified by the Columban missionary drive – introducing Christianity for a second time, but this time Christianity through the familiar Celtic ethnicity and Gaelic language. While St Ninian continued to be venerated, the Church in the islands became an off-shoot of the Irish Celtic Church. It looked to the centres of Celtic Christianity. It is around this time that the Ogham alphabet appears both in Ireland and in Orkney and Shetland, demonstrating the cultural links that existed between the two. The Church in the islands looked especially to the three missionary centres of Celtic Christianity: Iona, Inchcolm and Lindisfarne. Iona on Scotland's west coast was at first a stopping off point for travel to Ireland, but later a beacon of scholarship in its own right, a great pilgrimage centre, and the hallowed ground in which countless rulers of the north were buried. Iona could be reached direct by sea, though by braving the storms of Cape Wrath and the difficulty of a sharp direction change in an early ship. The alternative route via the Cromarty Firth and the Great

Glen – the route used by St Columba – required several changes of boat. Alternatively, Inchcolm in the Firth of Forth on the east coast was more accessible from Orkney and Shetland. Accessible too was Lindisfarne off the Northumberland coast, founded from Iona as the missionary centre for the newly emerging English nation. Orkney and Shetland had a Celtic church, language and culture with an Early English minority; Lindisfarne had a Celtic church, but spoke English and had an English culture, and had a Celtic minority. The two areas balance one another. We know that the Lindisfarne community knew about Orkney and Shetland, and contact between the two areas occurred. The Early English in Orkney and Shetland were not so very distant from their relatives within the Kingdom of Northumbria.

The Early English Kingdom of Northumbria was the most dynamic of the Anglo-Saxon kingdoms. At its zenith it boasted prosperity and internal security, a nascent democracy, and scholarship that was then among the best in the world. Its kings pursued an expansionist policy which not only increased the territory of Northumbria but led to their claiming overlordship over the whole of Britain, expressed through the title *Bretwalder* – ruler of Britain. Northumbria itself was a merger of two kingdoms, Bernicia north of the River Tees, and Deira to the south. The combined kingdom had a southern frontier on the River Humber – Northumbria means simply 'north of the Humber' – and a western frontier which at its maximum reached the Irish Sea and may have included the Isle of Man. The northern boundary both of Northumberland and its predecessor Bernicia is less clear.

English settlement in Bernicia is very old. The Saxon mercenaries who fought for the Roman Empire along Hadrian's Wall had settled the area to the north of the Wall well before the Roman Empire fell. The Celtic kingdom that corresponds with today's Lothian and Borders regions had an Early English minority population well before AD 449, the traditional date of English migration to England. The late fifth and the sixth centuries saw a great influx of English to this area, so that its character changed from a Celtic kingdom to an Anglo-Saxon kingdom. Edinburgh was founded by the English king Edwin, and was an integral part of English Northumbria. Nor is the Firth of Forth a northern boundary for Bernicia. The English influence and at times English rule extended well to the north. Thus, for example, early stone carving from Brechin in Angus shows unmistakable Northumbrian cultural influence, leaving little doubt that the Early English had reached as far north as Angus.

The Early English community in Orkney and Shetland from the late fifth century had contact with other English settlers located as little distance to the south as Angus. They also had contact across the North Sea with the Norwegians, the ancestors of the Vikings. They would have seen themselves not as English and Norwegians, or even as Orcadians and Shetlanders, but rather as one people, speaking dialects of one language. Archaeology has copious evidence of cultural contact across the North Sea at this time, but one example will suffice to illustrate it. In the Orkney Museum, Kirkwall, is exhibited a pre-Viking-age comb made from antler in a style characteristic of Orkney. It is like very many other antler combs that have been found, save that this one is made from reindeer antler. Reindeer do not occur on Orkney and Shetland or anywhere in the British Isles – and the antler must therefore be an import from Norway.

Towards the end of the eighth century these contacts across the North Sea became more frequent. In Norway a boat-builder had hit upon a marvellously improved manner of constructing ships. All boats up till then used the construction technique of a frame around which the ship was constructed. The results were heavy, and not suited for travel away from land. The new innovation – a stroke of genius – was to dispense with the frame, and build the ship from wood shaped so that each plank supported the next. The result is termed clinker building, and is the way in which timber boats are still constructed. The Norwegian invention created the longship, and brought about the Viking age. For Orkney and Shetland it brought the islands within no more than twenty-four hours' sailing of Norway, making frequent contact inevitable. It was the Early English population in Orkney and Shetland, speaking virtually the same language as the Vikings, who benefited most from this contact.

1.6 THE VIKINGS

The migration which had greatest impact on Orkney and Shetland is that of the Vikings. Today the islands see their Viking or Norse heritage as the feature which distinguishes them from mainland Scotland and the rest of the United Kingdom. Great though the impact of the Viking migration was, there is a tendency in popular culture to exaggerate its importance. In terms of the present-day ethnic mix of the islands the Vikings are a minority, and while many traditional strands in the islands' culture go back to the Vikings, much is from other sources.

The old theory – which still has some support in popular culture – was that the Vikings 'overwhelmed' Orkney and Shetland – a euphemism for a supposed genocide where through slaughter and enslavement the Vikings cleared the islands of all indigenous people. This was once seen as the explanation for the absence of pre-Norse place-names. Today we must discount this theory entirely, as genetic evidence shows that the pre-Norse people are the majority of the ethnic composition of the islands today. There was no genocide. We have identified no major battle sites, and the archaeological record shows many examples of Pictish and Viking culture side by side. Rather than overwhelming the Picts, the Viking migration was one of integration.

History records exact dates for the first Viking settlement of the Faroes, Iceland and Greenland. There is no comparable precision for the start of Viking settlement of either Orkney or Shetland, though many popular accounts give either AD 790 or 800, which look like exact dates. There was no simple start date. The Norse had a presence in both island groups well before 790, probably centuries before. They may have been encouraged by Pictish and Irish attacks on Orkney, which would have weakened the communities and made them vulnerable to Norse adventurers. The *Irish Annals of Tigernach* state that the Pictish High King Bridei MacBile 'destroyed' Orkney in AD 682, while the *Annals of Ulster* describe an Irish attack in 709. From around 790 the islands experienced a period of constant raiding by Viking adventurers, a situation which would have led first to accidental over-wintering of Viking bands, who found it easier to extort food and shelter from the native population than to return to Norway and a winter for which they were unprovided. Settlement followed, but was sporadic. So while variously 790 and 800 are frequently given as the start of the Viking age in Orkney and Shetland, we should accept that the records really do not give this sort of precision. There were some Norse in the islands before then, and still only a few in the early years of the ninth century.

In AD 875 King Harald I (Fair Hair) of Norway made a formal annexation of the islands to his kingdom, enforcing his claim with military action. The need for a naval expedition demonstrates the tenacious Viking influence prior to this time, and it is really only from 875 that we can regard the Vikings as truly in control of the islands. King Harald I cemented his control through creating a Jarl – an Earl – as governor of the islands, with the title Jarl of Orkney, a title which continued through to 1231. The Jarls of Orkney ruled Shetland as well as Orkney.

Politically there are two recurrent trends in the Norse governance of the islands: jarls had considerable independence from Norway, and jarls had to fight for their succession, usually with help from the king of Norway. The considerable independence that the jarl had from his nominal overlord the king of Norway had the effect that when there was a strong jarl in Orkney he was effectively an independent prince, and some in fact played Norway off against Scotland to their own benefit. However, such strong jarls were but few. The succession as jarl was on a hereditary principle, in as much as the jarls all came from one family, but modified with the idea that only an individual who could command the loyalty of the warriors could ever in fact rule. As a result jarls had to seize their earldom by force. Typically, succession went not from father to son – jarls tended to die young, and their young sons could not command the necessary respect and power – but rather from brother to brother or cousin to cousin. The succession was often disputed. Very often two or even three jarls were established simultaneously, and while there are examples of co-operation, warfare was far more common. Frequently Orkney and Shetland had for a time rival jarls, both claiming the title Jarl of Orkney, which implied jarl of both island groups. For support the rival jarls looked to their nominal overlord, the king of Norway. Time after time the kings of Norway sought to increase their own power by supporting the weaker jarl, with the intention of installing a jarl who would be a puppet dependent on their support.

The intrigues and battles are set out in the *Orkneyingasaga*. This magnificent story was written in Iceland around 1200, and preserved in the Flateyjarbok codex, a manuscript dating from around 1390 and found on the Icelandic island of Flatey. While it must be treated with care as a historic document, it does capture the spirit of the Viking age in Orkney and Shetland, where constant warfare was a fact of life, and where the heroic ethic of the Viking way of life displayed some of its finest characteristics.

How much the feuding of their leaders affected the farmers and fishers of the islands is a matter for debate. To a great extent they must have stayed separate from it. The *Orkneyingasaga* says almost nothing about the settled population, who played no part in most of the events of the mobile Vikings of the saga.

However, in some spheres of life the effect of the Viking age was clearly massive. The people lost their Celtic language and adopted a Germanic tongue, the ancestor of Orkney and Shetland Norn. They also lost their place-names. Today almost all place-names are of Norse origin, suggesting a thorough cultural replacement. England has not had a Celtic-speaking population for well over a thousand years, yet Celtic place-names are common still, and even names from pre-Celtic languages have in some cases survived. By contrast Orkney and Shetland experienced an almost total loss of their old place-names, a startling phenomenon which seems as yet without an adequate explanation. The missionary drives associated first with St Ninian and later with St Columba had made the islands Christian, but Christianity seems to have been lost at the start of the Viking age, at least as the faith of the majority. Worship of the Norse gods was introduced – as shown by their names in place-names – and Christianity declined, though it did survive, as for example the continued veneration of St Ninian indicates. The islands were nominally re-converted in AD 995 by Olav Tryggvasson, though his motive was more political than apostolic, and his visit little more than a stop-off on a voyage from Ireland to Norway. It is a clear century later that the martyrdom of Earl Magnus and his beatification as St Magnus shows evidence of popular Christianity, and with the twelfth-century building of St Magnus' Cathedral and many other churches we can regard both island groups as Christian.

Throughout the period of the Viking jarls it seems most appropriate to regard the islands as a Pictish–Celtic population which had a Viking ruling class imposed upon it. It is not at all clear that the people would have regarded themselves as Norse, and it is interesting to see that on the extinction of the Viking jarls in 1231 the islands were given to a Pictish overlord, the Mormaer (or Earl) of Caithness, a decision which may have reflected the reality of a perceived Pictish cultural and ethnic identity. Caithness itself acknowledged the king of Norway as overlord, and like Orkney and Shetland had experienced substantial Viking influence, but Caithness still retained the trappings of Pictish governance. Increasingly the rule of the islands came from the south, and direct Norwegian influence waned. Ultimately the islands were in reality and often in law part of two systems, as exemplified by their Earl Henry Sinclair. Created Jarl of Orkney in 1379 by the King of Norway Haakon VI (Magnusson) he clearly accepted the king of Norway as his overlord, and is often credited with the rank of prince in the Norwegian system, so Prince of Orkney. He was also, however, an earl in the Scottish system, accepting the king of Scots as his overlord, and with extensive lands in Scotland. The reality is that Orkney and Shetland had considerable de facto independence, and when Norway itself became part of the kingdom of Denmark and the centre of power shifted south to Copenhagen, the rule of the islands from the new Scandinavian capital became ever more notional.

The end of the Norwegian period is conveniently dated as 1468, when King Christian I of Denmark gave the islands to the king of Scotland as payment of a dowry for his daughter Margaret, who married King James III of Scots. This political handover reflects a real shift in geo-politics, which had put the islands well within the orbit of Scotland, and with marginal Danish control. The last Jarl of Orkney was given lands in Scotland to relinquish his claim, and from 1471 the islands may be regarded as an integral part of the kingdom of Scotland.

1.7 THE SCOTS

The coming of the Scots is a steady migration over centuries. There were Scots in Orkney and Shetland long before the islands were given to Scotland as the 1468 dowry of Margaret of Norway, and Norse in the islands well after. The ascendancy of Scottish people and with them the English language was a slow process. English at this time is the English of the court of the Scottish Stewart kings, and the English brought to Orkney and Shetland is in origin a series of related east-coast Lowland Scots dialects. The English of the islands owes much to Leith and Aberdeen, and very little to Highland Scots.

In language terms the most significant event was the use of the English-language Bible and Prayer Book, the Bible from 1611 being the Authorised Version of King James, I of England and VI of Scots. Though just eight years had passed since the accession of King James VI of Scots to the throne of England had brought about the union of the crowns of England and Scotland, the whole of Scotland (including Orkney and Shetland) was looking south for its standard language. The English spoken in Orkney and Shetland was beginning to be influenced not by any Scottish dialect but by London. The position of English as the language of religion, and therefore also as the language of literacy, ensured its success. We know that the Lord's Prayer was available in Orkney and Shetland Norn, and therefore someone at some time must have translated it, though whether from English, Norwegian or even Latin or Greek we cannot know. It is just possible that some other parts of the Bible were available in Orkney and Shetland Norn. However, the Bible used in church was the English Bible.

The Scots migration had brought first the dialect and culture of Lowland Scotland to the islands, and subsequently much linguistic and cultural influence from further south. The heritage of many Lowland Scots dialects may be heard in the islands, and many of the features which today seem distinctive of the islands' way of speaking are in fact rather recent imports. The port of Leith has been a particular source of migrants, and therefore a major force in the modern dialects.

Over the many strands of the linguistic heritage of the islands has been imposed the southern English standard, brought to Orkney and Shetland as to every corner of the United Kingdom.

2

Historical Records

WHEN EXAMINING RECORDS of the earliest history of Orkney and Shetland we are looking not at primary sources, but at comments made by early historians. Historians of the classical world and the early Middle Ages are particularly prone to retelling stories with an interpretation that seems to them to make better sense of the history they had, or to point a moral which had relevance for their own day. Nevertheless, they usually told what they believed to be true, and frequently demonstrate an ethical code which promoted truth telling. All early histories must be treated with caution, but equally cannot be discounted simply because they are old. When a historian states that the Early English were in Orkney and Shetland, it is right for us to be cautious, but wrong to discount this statement without good reason. The recent consensus has been to discount such references, in my view without good reason, and perhaps for no reason other than that the historical accounts do not fit present-day cultural aspirations. At the least the historical records establish a plausible hypothesis that the Early English were in Orkney and Shetland – as they state – and we should look for a way to test this hypothesis.

Many of the early references to Orkney and Shetland are tantalisingly brief. They tell us little more than that the islands were known to the writer. They were on the map – quite literally so, as the map in Claudius Ptolemy's *Geographica* dating from about AD 150 marks them as two distinct archipelagos. Interestingly, Ptolemy divides the two groups, while many classical writers treat them as one.

Ptolemy was drawing on Mediterranean knowledge of the islands which stretched back around five centuries. Centuries before and after his age, the islands were known. The accounts of Orkney and Shetland from the ancient world and the early Middle Ages which have been preserved are few, but this should not be taken to imply that they did not exist. Rather, the paucity of accounts is a result of the chances of survival. Orkney and Shetland were known and what information is given is real, often with an indication of the original informant.

2.1 DIODORUS SICULUS

The earliest surviving account is a report by Diodorus Siculus, a Greek historian writing around 49 BC. His world is far removed from Orkney and Shetland: born in Sicily, he lived most of his life in Egypt, and made a number of journeys around the Mediterranean and the Near East which provided the materials for his history. He published his life's work in the monumental *Bibliotheca Historia* (*Historical Library*) of forty volumes, assembling work from numerous older historians, around a dozen of whom can be identified today. Key to evaluating the work of Diodorus Siculus is the understanding that he was not an original writer but rather an assembler of other people's works, as he acknowledged himself by calling his writings a library. The quality is as good or as bad as his sources, and he does almost nothing to evaluate the relative strengths of these sources. His lack of critical judgement extends even to contradictory statements within the space of a few pages, where two different sources have said something different and both are quoted by him. Diodorus Siculus may rightly be regarded as a poor historian, but he is nonetheless a good archivist, who has preserved material that would otherwise have been lost. We may reasonably criticise his lack of synthesis, but can still value his individual sources.

The material he presents on Orkney comes from a now-lost account which he found describing a voyage by a Greek sailor Pytheas living in the Greek colony of Marseilles. Pytheas, whose information dates from around 330 BC, stands at the forefront of the classical world's geographical knowledge of the British Isles and of much of Northern Europe. His work was nearly three centuries old when Diodorus Siculus was reading it. As copied by Diodorus Siculus, Pytheas gives us much information which is verifiable, leading to a reasonable assumption that he had sound sources. He gives a brief description of Britain, and mentions in a paragraph lands to the north of Britain, variously identified by scholars with Norway, Iceland and even Greenland. His knowledge is believed to come from familiarity with the tin trade routes, which in his day connected the Mediterranean with Cornwall. This trade route was exceptionally long for its day – from Pytheas' home in Marseilles through the western Mediterranean, the Straits of Gibraltar, north along the coast of Iberia, and across the Bay of Biscay to Brittany and to Cornwall – yet it has left archaeological traces which leave no doubt that these voyages were a regular feature, just as they were described. There is no difficulty in believing that Pytheas made a journey as far as Cornwall, or spoke with people who had made such a journey, but Cornwall is still a long way from Orkney. The tin trade route ended in Cornwall, and the Greeks had no reason based on trade to go further north. While the possibility must in theory exist that the Greeks made a voyage of exploration north from Cornwall, there is absolutely nothing to support this idea. Rather, it

seems that Pytheas of Marseilles had a local source for his description
of points to the north, presumably a source in Cornwall or Ireland or
elsewhere in Celtic Britain.

The Orkney Islands are named in the account as 'Orkan Akroterion'. The word *akroterion* means promontory or headland, but
within the context of Diodorus Siculus and other Greek writers, the
term means the extreme point of a mass of land including offshore
islands – there is no contradiction in calling the Orkney Islands by
this name. Most interesting is the proper noun Orkan. The final
-an is a regular Greek suffix, stripped of which the name is simply
Ork. Early Irish writers used for Orkney the name Inse Orc, Orc
Islands, and the use of an identical term by Pytheas suggests that he
had Irish or other Celtic informants, and that his intelligence was
good. Around 330 BC the Greeks knew that there were islands at the
northern extremity of Britain, and knew that they were called Ork.
The Orkney Islands were in the history books.

2.2 CLAUDIUS CLAUDIANUS

A most striking classical source is the one which places the English
in the Orkney Islands in AD 363. Our author is Claudius Claudianus, writing in AD 398 about a voyage made in 363 by the then
Roman general and later Roman emperor Theodosius.

Claudius Claudianus cannot be regarded as one of the great
literary figures of his age. He writes in verse, most of it not very
good, and often at encyclopaedic length. He is a Greek writing in
Latin, not his mother tongue, and it shows. Furthermore, many
of his works glorify the achievements of Theodosius, one of the
late emperors and a figure who has generally not captured the
enthusiasm of later generations. As a result the works of Claudius
Claudianus are little read, and today even a recent edition of his
substantial output is lacking. Notwithstanding his literary short-
comings, historians have found him a sound source. While capa-
ble of leaving out events which were unfavourable to Theodosius,

he seems to have taken considerable pains to get his facts right for those events which he did report. In the end he was writing for a court audience who would have known the facts. With this in mind, when he mentions the Orkney Islands we should take his comments seriously. The key lines (from *De IV Consulatu Honorii Augusti*) are:

> quid rigor aeternus,
> caeli quid frigora prosunt ignotumque fretum?
> maduerunt Saxone fuso Orcades;
> incaluit Pictorum sanguine Thyle;
> Scottorum cumulos flevit glacialis Hiverne.

The accepted translation into English is:

> What avail against him [Theodosius] the eternal snows, the frozen air, the uncharted sea? The Orcades ran red with Saxon slaughter; Thule was warm with the blood of Picts; ice-bound Hibernia wept for the heaps of slain Scots. (Claudian, trans. M. Platnauer, Loeb Classical Library (London, 1922), vol. 2, §8)

One translation note can be added to this. The translator sanitises the slaughter of the Saxons – the word in Latin is 'poured out' and the sense seems to be 'disembowelled', suggesting a particularly violent death, even a ritual slaughter.

A few contextual notes can also be added. Theodosius' voyage is accepted as historical fact; all Claudius Claudianus does for us is fill out some details. In AD 363 the Scots were of course living in Ireland (their migration to Scotland is much later); Thule is used by Claudius Claudianus here and elsewhere for Scotland north of the Forth–Clyde Valley; Orcades are used by him and other Roman writers for both Orkney and Shetland together.

The term 'Saxon' is unremarkable. Tacitus in his *Germania* presents a catalogue of names of Germanic tribes. Three he links together: the Jutes, Angles and Saxons. Of these the Jutes are the smallest group, and are quickly found to be called Saxons. Angles and Saxons are virtual synonyms, often linked in the form Anglo-Saxon. If there is a difference at all, it is that the Saxons later settled in the south of Britain, and the Angles in the north, yet even this difference is not consistent. The Romans chose just one term to describe all the Anglo-Saxon people – Saxons. In time the people too used just one term, Angles or English. We can follow the Romans and call these settlers by the name the Romans used, or we can use the name that has been adopted in English: the Early English.

The Romans knew very clearly whom they meant by the term Saxons. The Saxons are the Germanic people then living around the Rhine Estuary in north-west Europe, and who were harrying much of southern and eastern England. The Saxons were the English. What Claudius Claudianus gives us is a statement that the English were living in Orkney in AD 363, and in sufficient numbers to be worthy opponents for the great General Theodosius.

Claudius Claudianus has sometimes been dismissed on the grounds that there must surely be some mistake. Yet he is not the sole source, and language supports his position. He needs to be taken seriously.

2.3 PLINY, TACITUS, JUVENAL, ISIDORE

Several other classical writers mention Orkney, by which they are usually considered to mean both Orkney and Shetland.

Typically, early reports are little more than the name of the islands. This, for example, is the sort of reference found in Book IV of the *Natural History* (about AD 77) of Gaius Plinius Secundus – Pliny the Elder – a man whose curiosity killed him when in 79 he sailed into the Bay of Naples to see the eruption of Vesuvius at close quarters. Writing of Orkney, he states: 'sunt autem XL Orcades, modicis inter se discretae spatiis' (There are 40 Orkney Islands, separated from one another with small spaces in between).

Tacitus also mentions the islands. Remembered today for the *Agricola* and *Germania* – his account of the life of his uncle Agricola and his description of the Germanic peoples – Tacitus makes the statement that in AD 83 (or possibly 84 – the dating is unclear) a fleet led by Agricola 'discovered and subdued previously unknown islands called the Orcades'. He is, of course, wrong in regarding the Orkney Islands as 'previously unknown', as Pliny clearly knew of them a decade before, and Pytheas four centuries before. Perhaps Tacitus means previously unvisited by Romans.

Juvenal, writing early in the second century AD, also mentions the Orkney Islands – and specifically denies that Theodosius conquered them.

> Arma quidem ultra
> litora Juvernae promovimus et modo captas
> Orcades, et minima contentos nocte Britannos.
> > *Satire* 2.159–61

> Our army we have advanced beyond the shores of Ireland, beyond the recently captured Orkneys, where the Britons contend with very short nights.

This fits our understanding of the Theodosian voyage around Britain as part of an attempted conquest of the north of Britain which failed.

Among later Latin writers, St Isidore, Archbishop of Seville (560–636) also mentions the Orkney Islands. In his encyclopaedic *Origines* (14.6.5) he states: 'Orcades insulae Oceani intra Britanniam positae numero triginta tres, quarum viginti desertae sunt, tredecim coluntur' (The Orkneys are thirty-three islands of the Ocean situated within Britain, of which twenty are deserted and thirteen inhabited). Presumably he has a source which encourages him to change Ptolemy's forty to thirty-three.

While it would be pleasing to have more information, it is clear that the classical world knew of the islands and knew something about them.

2.4 NENNIUS

An early medieval account of Orkney and corroboration of the Saxon presence there is provided by the writings identified with the Welsh monk Nennius.

Nennius himself is a shadowy figure. The year of his death is usually considered to be AD 809, with his writing traditionally dated to the first decade of the ninth century, therefore the last years of his life. Some doubt has recently been expressed as to whether the writings attributed to him are really by him, or instead by an anonymous author and wrongly attributed to him.

Whether written by Nennius or an anonymous writer, *Historia Brittonum* provides an account of early British history from the Celtic British perspective, and includes both factual material and much that is regarded today simply as myth. For example, the earliest references to King Arthur and Merlin come from Nennius, and it is Merlin who in Nennius is considered responsible for moving the stones of Stonehenge to Salisbury plain and erecting them there by magic. Among such mythical stories is nonetheless much history, particularly in the later periods, and where we are able to check Nennius from other sources for these later periods he is usually right.

Nennius provides four references to Orkney, set out below, with discussion following.

- Three considerable islands belong to Britain; one, on the south, opposite the Armorican shore, called Wight; another between Ireland and Britain, called Eubonia or Man; and another directly north, beyond the Picts, named Orkney; and hence it was anciently a proverbial expression, in reference to its kings and rulers, 'He reigned over Britain and its three islands.' (*History of Britain* 8, trans. J.A. Giles, London, 1848)
- After an interval of not less than eight hundred years, came the Picts, and occupied the Orkney Islands: whence they laid waste many regions, and seized those on the left-hand side of Britain,

where they still remain, keeping possession of a third part of Britain to this day. (*History of Britain* 12)

- The second after him, who came into Britain, was the emperor Claudius, who reigned forty-seven years after the birth of Christ. He carried with him war and devastation; and, though not without loss of men, he at length conquered Britain. He next sailed to the Orkneys, which he likewise conquered, and afterwards rendered tributary. No tribute was in his time received from the Britons; but it was paid to British emperors. He reigned thirteen years and eight months. His monument is to be seen at Moguntia (among the Lombards), where he died on his way to Rome. (*History of Britain* 21)

- Hengist, after this, said to Vortigern, 'I will be to you both a father and an adviser; despise not my counsels, and you shall have no reason to fear being conquered by any man or any nation whatever; for the people of my country are strong, warlike, and robust: if you approve, I will send for my son and his brother, both valiant men, who at my invitation will fight against the Picts, and you can give them the countries in the north, near the wall called Gual.' The incautious sovereign having assented to this, Octa and Ebusa arrived with forty ships. In these they sailed round the country of the Picts, laid waste the Orkneys, and took possession of many regions, even to the Pictish confine beyond the Frenesic Sea. (*History of Britain* 38)

Nennius distinguishes between the islands of Britain and Ireland, and his Britain does not mean the British Isles but rather Britain without Ireland. His position of the islands of Wight, Man and Orkney is broadly correct, though the importance of these three comparatively small islands to early British rulers is surprising and not corroborated elsewhere. At least he shows awareness that Orkney exists, even if he regards it as a single island. His statement that the Picts occupied Orkney is correct – with the proviso that he is referring to the second Celtic phase of Pictish culture – and furthermore shows an awareness that the Celtic Picts were not the indigenous people of the islands. His statement that this happened eight hundred years after an earlier event might give hope of a date for the Celtic Pictish invasion, but the earlier event is mythical and without a fixed date, so this does not help. His 'third part' of Britain occupied by the Picts reflects his statement that Britain was divided between the Britons, the English and the Picts. It would be a mistake to equate a 'third part' with one-third; rather he means one of three.

His final reference to Orkney comes within a paragraph which requires some commentary. Hengist is a historical figure, who with his brother Horsa (a rather more shadowy figure) led the English invasion of Kent in AD 449. Nennius says that the Orkney expedition took place in 443. Vortigern is likewise a historical figure, the British king at the time who invited Hengist and Horsa as mercenaries to fight with him against the Picts. Hengist's promise to Vortigern sounds plausible as the sort of promise a mercenary leader might make, and in the event history indeed remembers Vortigern as 'incautious', because his mercenaries turned against him, defeating him and occupying his land. 'Gual' in this paragraph is the Antonine Wall – the Firth–Clyde valley that was the southern boundary of the Picts; the Frenesic Sea has been plausibly identified with the Solway Firth, and implies that the Picts were found in areas south of the Antonine Wall, an implication supported by archaeology.

There is nothing in the references Nennius makes to Orkney that is demonstrably wrong, and much that we know is right.

The army of Hengist is defined as mercenary – a band of hired soldiers. Their attack on the Picts is at variance with alliances which at one time existed between the Saxons and Picts against the Romans. In his later conduct Hengist turned against Vortigern, fighting against his former ally. There is no settled allegiance for this group. The attack on Orkney by forty Saxon ships demonstrates the ease with which the Saxons could voyage to the northern extreme of the North Sea. Ship construction had changed little in the last century or so, and if Hengist could take forty ships to Orkney his ancestors certainly had the capability so to do.

The event described is a Saxon attack on Orkney, not a settlement. The importance of the account is that it demonstrates that the Saxons reached Orkney. Elsewhere we know that they settled wherever they could, and indeed the next century and a half of British history was to be dominated by their settlement. It is a reasonable hypothesis that Saxons reaching Orkney would have settled there.

2.5 THE ANGLO-SAXON CHRONICLE

The English settlement in Kent is described within the terse narrative of the *Anglo-Saxon Chronicle*, which presents a year-by-year history of England. The relevant entries describe the efforts of leaders of the Roman province of Britain to keep order. Following the fall of the imperial capital of Rome in AD 410 Roman Britain did continue as an autonomous Roman province, with Roman law and culture, with nominal Roman emperors claiming to rule, and British client kings. In these extracts we see Marcian and Valentinus as supposed emperors, and Vortigern as a British client king who would in theory have given his allegiance to these representatives of Rome.

449. In this year Mauricius and Valentinian obtained the kingdom and reigned seven years. In their days Hengest and Horsa, invited by Vortigern, king of the Britons, came to Britain at a place which is called Ebbsfleet, at first to help the Britons, but later they fought against them. The king ordered them to fight against the Picts, and so they did and had victory wherever they came. They then sent to Angel; ordered [them] to send them more aid and to be told of the worthlessness of the Britons and of the excellence of the land. They then sent them more aid. These men came from three nations of Germany: from the Old Saxons, from the Angles, from the Jutes. From the Jutes came the people of Kent and the people of the Isle of Wight, that is the race which now dwells in the Isle of Wight, and the race among the West Saxons which is still called the race of the Jutes. From the Old Saxons came the East Saxons and South Saxons and West Saxons. From Angel, which has stood waste ever

since between the Jutes and the Saxons, came the East Angles, Middle Angles, Mercians, and all the Northumbrians.

455. In this year Hengest and Horsa fought against king Vortigern at a place which is called Aylesford, and his brother Horsa was slain. And after that Hengest succeeded to the kingdom and Aesc, his son.

457. In this year Hengest and Aesc fought against the Britons at a place which is called Crayford, and there slew four thousand men; and the Britons then forsook Kent and fled to London in great terror.

465. In this year Hengest and Aesc fought against the Welsh near Wippedesfleot and there slew twelve Welsh nobles and one of their thanes, whose name was Wipped, was slain there.

473. In this year Hengest and Aesc fought against the Welsh and captured innumerable spoils, and the Welsh fled from the English like fire. (*The Anglo-Saxon Chronicle*, trans. G.N. Garmondsway, London and Melbourne, 1984)

There is no reason to doubt the accuracy of the account presented. The genealogy of Hengist and Horsa goes back to Woden (Odin), not the pagan god, but a Germanic king who happened to bear the name of the god, so a mythical divine descent is not being claimed for Hengist and Horsa. Although we have no way of proving the genealogy set out, there is no reason to disbelieve it. The names of the brothers mean 'stallion' and 'horse', and are of a type of name used by early Germanic peoples. The English invasion of Britain took place around the years specified and started in Kent, and the basic division between Jutes, Angles and Saxons set out by the account is corroborated by linguistic evidence. We do not have archaeological evidence for battles in Kent at Aylesford and Crayford, but this is no reason for doubting they took place. Wippedfleet has not been certainly identified. Other early sources corroborate the account in the *Anglo-Saxon Chronicle*, particularly the works of Bede, a particularly careful and reliable historian from the early Middle Ages. The Britons certainly lost battles against the invading English, and the death toll of 4,000 at Crayford, very high for a battle at this time, is in keeping with the general thrust of the rapid English advance. The remnants of the British armed forces fell back, while the British people who remained accepted rule by the English.

English history therefore begins with Hengist and Horsa, and rightly so. In the year AD 449 England started.

Yet Nennius has shown us that Hengist is as much a figure for Orkney as for England. It was Hengist who in 443 'wasted' the Orkneys. The contribution of the *Anglo-Saxon Chronicle* is to provide confirmation that Hengist is a real figure who six years later was leading a group of mercenaries in the hire of the Roman governor of Britain.

2.6 ICELANDERS

Iceland is a rich repository of the medieval culture of the Germanic North Atlantic, including Orkney and Shetland. In Northern Europe as a whole, little has survived. Old English, for example, has just four manuscript codices of literature – about 30,000 lines in total – while for Old High German we have only a few fragments of literature, and for Gothic and a host of other Germanic languages no literature has survived. In contrast to the four literary manuscripts of Old English, Old Icelandic can boast 1,666 literary manuscripts. This amazing survival demonstrates the care over the centuries given to books in Iceland – or perhaps the carelessness in most of Northern Europe. So great is the volume of Icelandic material that it is worth examining it for references to Orkney and Shetland.

The results are actually disappointing. Perhaps three of the manuscripts may be directly linked with Orkney, in that they were probably composed there. These are *The Lay of Kraka*, *The Lay of the Joms-Vikings* and *The Proverb Poem*, the last two apparently written by a Bishop of Orkney, Bjarni Kolbeinsson. They tell us almost nothing about the islands. *The Lay of the Joms-Vikings* sets out the story of a Viking military order established not in Orkney but on the southern shore of the Baltic Sea around the Oder estuary, and perhaps demonstrates the international interests of the islands.

Snorri Sturluson (1178–1241) produced an encyclopaedic book which charted the geography, history and religion of the northern world. It is known to us as *Heimskringla* (*The Orb of the World*) from its opening words (which incidentally make it clear that he knew the world to be a sphere). In his account both Orkney and Shetland are mentioned, though there is little information provided. The most frequent references are to Orkney, which has approaching two dozen references, as opposed to Shetland, which is mentioned just half a dozen times. There are references to the politics and history of the islands, as well as incidental references, for example to Icelandic crusaders to Jerusalem who travelled via Orkney. Snorri regarded Orkney and Shetland as being so local to Iceland that he did not provide the sort of background information about them that he provides for more distant lands.

The picture that emerges is of an Orkney and Shetland completely integrated within the Viking world, well known to Icelanders, who themselves took an interest in events elsewhere in Northern Europe.

2.7 ARCHAEOLOGY

Archaeology provides a test for much of the story told by the early historians. Victorian schoolroom history followed the early historians and taught that in AD 449 the two brothers, Hengist and Horsa, landed in Kent as the first English settlers in the British Isles. Today we have to put back by at least a couple of hundred years the first English presence in England. The Roman 'Saxon Shore' of Kent and Sussex is now accepted as being as much a series of trading posts as defensive structures. A Saxon settlement of the fourth century has been excavated on the banks of the Thames.

The Romans record the Saxons trading and raiding in the fourth century right up the east coast of England as far as Roman power went, and it is perfectly reasonable to see the Saxons raiding further north in Scotland.

For Orkney and Shetland it is credible that the invention of the longship made possible the Viking mass migrations that made these islands an integral part of the Norwegian Viking world, from around AD 790. But the date of the coming of the Vikings is as unclear from the archaeological record as it is from the historic. On the contrary, sites including Jarlshof suggest the possibility of what may be Norse settlement much earlier. As the Saxons and Vikings had a very similar material culture, Saxon settlement is equally in keeping with the archaeological record.

The site of Jarlshof clearly indicates the pattern of continuity of settlement exhibited throughout the islands. Situated towards the southern tip of Shetland Mainland, the site's archaeological remains were first exposed by a series of severe storms at the end of the nineteenth century, and excavated in stages throughout the twentieth century. Jarlshof has been settled for around 4,500 years – and indeed a settlement is there still today. This is one of the longest periods of continuous settlement of any site in northern Europe.

Jarlshof provides a bronze age settlement, presumably to be linked with the pre-Indo-European Picts. It has iron age remains linked with the later, Celtic-speaking Picts, including a broch. There are four habitations of an unusual design called wheelhouses, which date from the period AD 200–600, and which are regarded as belonging to the last phase of Pictish culture. There are Viking buildings in the form of longhouses of familiar Viking design, and testifying to Viking occupation for around 400 years. There are remains of a later medieval settlement, of the Scottish farmhouse or palace built there, as well as the present hotel. The story told by the remains is not of settlements which died and the site subsequently reoccupied, but rather of continuity of settlement.

The incoming Celtic speakers lived alongside the pre-Indo-European Picts; Pictish culture developed through the broch age to the wheelhouses without a break; the Vikings in their turn took up residence alongside the indigenous Celtic-speaking Picts; in time the Viking settlement became a medieval village and ultimately a Scottish farmstead. The big house, now a ruin, which Sir Walter Scott called Jarlshof (thereby giving the site its name) was built in the seventeenth century; the present hotel continues the record of settlement. Each settlement develops into the next; there is no abrupt transition.

Jarlshof tells a story supported by very many other archaeological sites in Orkney and Shetland: that is that settlement was continuous, with incomers living alongside and ultimately integrating within an existing community. The culture of the islands is not Pictish or Celtic or Viking or Scots but rather an amalgam of all these elements and more.

As the archaeological record shows development rather than abrupt change, it is very hard to give precise dates for migrations. Jarlshof shows that there were Vikings there in the ninth century; what it doesn't show – and no archaeological site shows – is a date for the coming of the Vikings. There is no abrupt cultural change around AD 790, rather the gradual development of an indigenous culture. As far as the archaeological record is concerned, there was no coming of the Vikings.

2.8 PLACE-NAMES

No Early English place-names have been identified in Orkney and Shetland. In view of the similarity between Old Norse and Old English, particularly the very old form of English spoken by the Early English, such place-names would be difficult to spot, and it is also the case that no one has looked very hard for them.

The place-names of both island groups bear witness to their Viking heritage, and to this heritage almost exclusively. Many Viking place-names have been modified under the influence of Lowland Scots or subsequent Anglicisation, but most are still recognisably Old Norse in their origin. Most would not be out of place in Norway or Iceland. In the Preface to his *Etymological Dictionary of the Norn Language in Shetland* Jakob Jakobsen commented:

> Every small hill, point, rock, dale, cleft, brook, piece of field or meadow, etc., bears its own name, and these names, with comparatively few exceptions have been handed down in Norn dialect. The small Isle of Fetlar, scarcely four square miles in area, contains about two thousand place-names, and the entire number of place-names of the isles no doubt exceeds five thousand.

Very few Celtic or Pictish names survive, a state of affairs which hints at the totality of the Viking dominance of the islands. A notable exception to the Viking place-name dominance is the element *Orc-* in Orkney, which is certainly at least as early as Celtic and possibly even earlier, though of uncertain meaning. Even here the Viking dominance asserts itself with addition of Germanic *-ey* for islands.

The evidence of place-names in Orkney and Shetland does not tell a story which is easy to interpret. We would expect multiple layers of names, including Celtic and Pictish, with the settlement history written in the place-names. This is the pattern in England, for example, where place-names which are Celtic, Anglo-Saxon and Viking are all preserved.

The near-total absence of pre-Viking names in Orkney and Shetland was once explained in terms of a complete depopulation by the original people. This view is not tenable today, as it conflicts with the genetic profile.

Scandinavia shows a similar preponderance of Norse names. For example, in central and southern Sweden virtually all names are from Norse sources, with almost no trace of the names of earlier peoples. In Iceland every name is Norse, though a small Celtic population existed before the Viking migration. We can see that there is a pattern found in several Viking lands of Norse names completely supplanting earlier names, and presumably a cultural explanation must be sought.

The Viking names on Orkney and Shetland are from the time of the Viking settlement, and are therefore in the Old Norse language. They are mostly not examples of Orkney and Shetland Norn. Celtic and Pictish place-names have been looked for, but with very disappointing results – they hardly exist. As far as I can discover no one has looked for Anglo-Saxon place-names.

A curious place-name form exists on the island of Unst in the names Saxa Vord, Saxa's Haa, Saxa's Baa and Saxa's Kettle. Saxa is identified in the area as a giant, Saxi (with change of final vowel), who lived on the hill (Vord) that bears his name. The story is that a giant called Herman living on nearby Hermaness Hill caught a whale and asked to borrow Saxi's kettle – Saxa's Kettle today – to cook it in. Saxi demanded half the whale in payment. They squabbled and threw giant-sized stones, one of which is called today Saxa's Baa. Perhaps we should look to the giants Saxi and Herman for etymology of the place-names. However, in other locations we find that myths are created years after the origin of the place-names to explain them when the real origin has been forgotten. It would be interesting to see what an open-minded specialist would make of an alternative identification of Saxa with Saxon, and even Herman with German. It would be likely that the incoming Norse would record a settlement of Early English through place-names, and that somewhere in Orkney and Shetland we should be able to find them. Perhaps thousands of place-names should be re-examined: whether or not an identification of Saxa with Saxon is tenable, this task needs to be done. Of course, if these particular place-names can be established as recording not the giant Saxi but the Early English, they place a site of Early English settlement at the northern tip of Unst, which is the northernmost land of the United Kingdom today.

2.9 GENETICS

There is reason for optimism that genetic profiling may one day shed light on the Early English settlement of Orkney and Shetland, and much else in the prehistory and early history of the islands. At the moment this is not possible. The results obtained by genetic testing in Orkney and Shetland are noteworthy, certainly different from elsewhere in the British Isles, but these results are hard to interpret, and do not necessarily support the popular conclusions drawn from them. Much of what has been presented in the popular press is sensational, and often contradictory. In particular, Orkney and Shetland have been proclaimed Viking nations on the basis of genetic results, yet the real result is that a majority Viking origin for the people of the islands has been disproved. Around a third of the samples have shown genes which are believed to be from the Vikings. Orkney and Shetland may indeed be one-third Viking; this same statistic demonstrates that they are two-thirds something else. Popular coverage of the story has virtually stated the reverse.

Work by the geneticists Stephen Oppenheimer and Brian Sykes (working independently) has indicated that the largest impact on the genetic stock of the whole of the British Isles is from prehistoric migrations, predominantly from Iberia and moving along the Atlantic coast of France and into the British Isles. This population pre-dates Celtic or Anglo-Saxon or Viking and is the genetic signature of the first inhabitants of the British Isles after the retreat of the ice sheets at the end of the last ice age. This nameless neolithic people have more influence on the genetic make up of the population of the whole of the British Isles than all later groups combined. Oppenheimer notes that this Iberian genetic signature accounts for anything from a low of 59 per cent and a high of 96 per cent of the British population – his low from Fakenham in Norfolk, and his high from Llangefni in North Wales. Typically 70–85 per cent of the British genetic signature is from these earliest inhabitants; figures are particularly high in the west and north of the British

Isles, and lowest in certain specific eastern locations. In effect all the indigenous population of Britain owes the greatest part of its genetic heritage to these neolithic settlers. Confusingly, the popular press has found a name for these neolithic settlers, and is using the term Celt. This makes sense if we use Celtic to mean all the people who were in Britain before the Romans, though not if we see Celtic in its usual sense as meaning just the descendants of the people who brought Celtic languages and culture to Britain. Celt in this sense actually means neolithic plus Celtic. As well as these neolithic or Celtic genes, the British people have some genes from later peoples, but remain overwhelmingly the descendants of the earliest inhabitants of the islands. This broad genetic picture is the same in Orkney and Shetland. Genetically the people of Orkney and Shetland are simply British.

Throughout the British Isles the genetic element which does not go back to Iberia is a minority signature, never more than 41 per cent of the population of any one area, and typically in the region of around just 10–15 per cent. This minority signature is predominantly Germanic, though other groups can be identified, including Jewish and Romany Gypsy signatures. Recently there has been work to split the Germanic element into on the one hand Anglo-Saxon and Danish Viking (taken together) and on the other hand Norwegian Viking. The idea has been much supported by the popular media and does have academic backing. Therefore the present state of belief is that in the British Isles there is a majority neolithic genetic signature, which includes the Celtic strand, two distinct Germanic genetic signatures, Anglo-Saxon-Dane and Norwegian Viking, and rare representation of some later migrants.

That there is a single Anglo-Saxon and Danish Viking signature is exactly what we would expect as the two groups were of one ethnicity. The Anglo-Saxon-Dane signature accounts for the majority of the non-neolithic genetic component in Britain. The Celts (however defined) and these Germanics were two clearly differentiated ethnic groups, and it makes good sense that these two different genetic profiles should exist. But there is also claimed to be a distinct Norwegian Viking signature. That such a distinct signature should exist is wholly puzzling, as ethnically the Danish and Norwegian Vikings, along with the Anglo-Saxons and others, were all one group, and contact between Norwegian Vikings and others was extensive. The concept of a distinctive Norwegian Viking genetic profile has been given considerable support by the BBC through the television series *Blood of the Vikings* and it is an idea which has become part of popularly understood history. A distinct gene marking ethnicity has been found in around 33 per cent of Orkney and Shetland samples. The same gene is found in around 20 per cent of Norwegian samples, leading to the suggestion that it must have originated in Norway, and therefore that it is the signature of the Norse Vikings. Curiously, the gene is found in 0 per cent of samples in Dublin, which was the largest Viking town, though it is found in many Scottish and English locations where we know the Vikings settled.

We have copious evidence from history, archaeology and language that the Danish and Norwegian Vikings, along with the Anglo-Saxons, were one ethnic group. Clearly a distinctive genetic marker has been found in Orkney and Shetland and in other areas where we believe the Norwegian Vikings to have settled; what in my view cannot be upheld is the view that this genetic marker represents Norwegian Vikings. There are two other peoples to whom this genetic signature could have belonged. One is to a pre-Viking culture in Scandinavia who we know from the archaeological record had contact with Orkney and Shetland. The other is the Picts, who settled in many of the areas the Norwegian Vikings later settled, and who we know had contact with Norway.

Typical figures given by surveys of ethnicity in Orkney and Shetland are that the original male population displaying what has been identified as the Viking genetic signature was around 55 per cent Norwegian Viking, while the female population was around 10 per cent Norwegian Viking. This suggests a male invasion of the islands, and fits well with popular views of the Vikings. Aggregating the male and female figures suggests that around a third of the genetic heritage of the islands is the Norwegian Viking signature – or whatever group this signature represents – which is the highest concentration of this signature anywhere in the British Isles. However, around two-thirds of the ethnic mix of Orkney and Shetland is something else.

2.10 HISTORY AND THE EARLY ENGLISH

The records are not copious, yet they are there. Several early writers show an awareness of the Orkneys, a few of Shetland, and some appear to use the name Orkney for both Orkney and Shetland. The islands were known in antiquity.

Rather little is said about who was living there. Nennius is aware of Picts, but save for his record we are struggling to find textual support for settlement by the indigenous people, so well represented by the archaeological record. Against this background it is especially noteworthy that two early sources – Claudius Claudianus and Nennius – both place the Early English (the Saxons) in Orkney and Shetland. Were we using only the historical sources, the two peoples we would place on the islands are the Picts and the Early English.

It is noteworthy that Claudius Claudianus and Nennius are completely unrelated sources. The first is a Greek writing in Latin and living in Egypt; the second is a Welsh-speaking monk, presumably living in Wales, and writing some four hundred years or more later. No one has suggested Claudius Claudianus as a source for Nennius – and even a casual reading shows no evidence for this. The references they make to Early English presence in the islands are at dates more than a century apart and in connection with completely different events.

Neither had a political reason for wishing to place the Early English in the islands, and both in different ways were writing for an audience that knew something of the matter discussed. Claudius Claudianus was effectively a court poet at a court where there were people who had personal knowledge of the events described.

Nennius – or the pseudo-Nennius – was writing in the milieu of a Wales suffering continued incursions from the English, and where the English enemy's age of settlement in Britain was part of popular folklore.

Add to these historical records which mention the Early English the support from both archaeology and place-names and a possibility emerges which deserves examination.

3

Confirmation from Language

THE HISTORICAL RECORD presents a working hypothesis that the Early English were present in Orkney and Shetland at least from the fourth century. However, the historical record rests primarily on brief notes by Claudius Claudianus and Nennius, and received wisdom today is that there must be some mistake in their statements. The problem seems to be that the earlier writers do very little more than state that the Early English were in the islands. There is no information about when they came, how they lived alongside other peoples in the islands, or what became of them. Perhaps too there is a lack of enthusiasm among many popular writers today about Orkney and Shetland for the idea of Early English settlement in what are being presented as almost Viking nations.

An earlier age gave greater credence to the testimony of the early historians. Thus in the 1797 edition of *Encyclopaedia Britannica* in the entry for Orkney is written:

58

In many places of the country we find round hillocks or barrows, here known by the name of *brogh*, signifying, in the Teutonic language, burying place, supposed to have been the cemeteries of the ancient Saxons . . . It has been asserted, that the Orkneys, as well as the hills of Shetland, were originally peopled from Norway, in the ninth, tenth, or eleventh century. Others again imagine, with as much probability, that the Picts were the original inhabitants, and call Orkney the ancient kingdom of the Picts. Certain singular houses, now overgrown with earth, are called *Picts houses*; and the Pentland firth (formerly *Pightland* or *Pictland*) is supposed to retain their name. Claudian's lines, cited by Mr Camden, prove, that the Picts, with some other German colony, particularly the Saxons, were at that time in possession of these isles; and so Ninnius expressly says.

This old statement remains largely valid (save that today *brogh* would not be considered a Saxon word). This is the conclusion that the records lead to: the Picts were present, then the Saxons or Early English came, then the Vikings. As late as 1965 Erik Linklater in his *Orkney and Shetland* states of the Saxons that they 'may have been recurrent visitors'. Yet subsequent writers have largely avoided the Early English, either passing over them in silence, or citing insufficient evidence. Thus a state of affairs has been reached where some form of proof of the early historians is needed. What past ages took on trust our age needs to have proved beyond reasonable doubt.

3.1 ORKNEY AND SHETLAND NORN

Through the Middle Ages the indigenous language of Orkney and Shetland was Orkney and Shetland Norn. The name is cumbersome, but a better term is not established. It is also misleading, as it is not the same as Norn (the later form of Old Norse), and while it is certainly similar to the Norn language it is more than just simply a dialect variant of that language which happens to be found in Orkney and Shetland. There is no evidence that its speakers called it Norn – indeed we don't really know what they called it – or that anyone else called it Norn. In many respects such names as 'Orcadian and Shetlandic' would be more appropriate, though they are ruled out because it has become customary to apply these terms to the English dialects of modern insular Scots spoken on Orkney and Shetland. 'Yaltmol' is recorded as a name for the language on Shetland – along with 'Yealtaland' for Shetland and 'Yalts' for Shetlanders – and were it better established might well have been a convenient name. Perhaps 'Old Orcadian' and 'Old Shetlandic' would be better – though I have stuck with the familiar 'Orkney and Shetland Norn'.

We know rather little about the language because it is extinct. From around 1400 the language declined steadily, so that by around 1800 it may be regarded as effectively dead. English dominated, and for many years English has been the sole language of the majority of inhabitants. The islands have lost their distinctive indigenous language, and with so few records of it we know little about it.

The traditional assumption is that Orkney and Shetland Norn was simply Norn. According to this school of thought, it is in origin the language spoken in Norway at the end of the eighth century at the beginning of the Viking age, and which was carried by the Vikings wherever they went. It is therefore the same language as Old Icelandic, Old Faroese, and a close relative of the modern Icelandic, Faroese, Norwegian, Danish and Swedish languages.

This definition for Orkney and Shetland Norn cannot be wholly set aside. The first Vikings who settled in Orkney and Shetland certainly spoke Norn, as did those who settled further west in the Faroe Islands, Iceland and Greenland, or south in the Hebrides, Ireland and England, or east through the great rivers of Russia. In the Viking age Norn was a single, unified language, the language of the Vikings. And Orkney and Shetland Norn certainly owes the majority of its vocabulary and grammar to the language of the Vikings.

However, as the Viking age came to an end the Norn language developed in different ways in different locations. Where there was contact between Viking groups and their successors, a uniform language was maintained; where there was isolation, different forms developed. Interference from other languages caused modifications too.

In Iceland it has traditionally been maintained that the Viking language remained with minimal changes, and Icelanders today take pride in their Viking heritage as exemplified by what they see as their unchanged language. Old Norse, or Old Icelandic as the Icelanders prefer to call it, is held to be little different from the modern language of Iceland. Perhaps inevitably this traditional view is somewhat overstated. In fact the language of Iceland has changed and developed over the thousand years since the Viking settlement, and modern Icelandic is not the same as Old Icelandic. Years of Danish influence have left their mark, while the relative isolation of Iceland has enabled idiosyncratic changes to happen. Nevertheless, Icelanders today can read Old Icelandic literature with only a few difficulties, and can reasonably claim to be speaking today something which is as close as exists anywhere to the language spoken by the Vikings. Something very like Norn is alive in Iceland today.

Yet the Icelandic model is unusual. Elsewhere the Norn language has undergone substantial changes, as it did in Orkney and Shetland.

In the Faroe Islands the language development has been complicated by the geographical isolation that exists between various islands in the Faroese group, and by the imposition of a foreign language – Danish – as the language of church and government. By the end of the nineteenth century the speech of the Faroe Islands had broken into a number of low-prestige dialects, sometimes sufficiently different for there to be real difficulties in communication, with Danish increasingly used in place of Faroese. It was only the intervention of scholars and teachers that established a Faroese linguistic standard and brought the language back from the brink. Faroese came about as close to language death as it is possible for a language to come and recover. Faroese today is based on scholarly work which consciously archaised the language, that is to say deliberately utilised old forms in order to find a standard. Faced with the plethora of mutually incomprehensible forms on the different islands in the archipelago there seemed to be no other practical solution if Faroese was to survive. In effect Faroese has been brought closer to its Norn roots, and therefore closer to the modern language of Iceland. A Viking would find the Faroese of the early twenty-first century far easier to understand than the language of the late nineteenth century. Icelanders and Faroese today can understand one another without too many difficulties, while 200 years ago the difficulties would have been greater. Faroese is a linguistic oddity, almost a re-creation of the language of nearly a thousand years ago.

In Scandinavia the Norn language was greatly changed in part by the influence of neighbouring German, and in part by constant contact between the peoples within Scandinavia that promoted similarities between the languages. It is customary to speak today of the three national languages of Danish, Norwegian and Swedish, but all are mutually intelligible, and without the political boundaries would be regarded as dialects of one language. For a European comparison it is possible to look at Italian, where today there are more differences between dialects than exist between the three Scandinavian languages, yet Italy is one nation with one written standard and therefore considers itself to have one language. In Scandinavia speakers of any one language can read and understand the others, though sometimes cultural identities lead to a tendency to maximise language differences. Danish and Norwegian in particular are so close today that many linguists insist they are one single Dano-Norwegian language. But while the Scandinavian languages are close to one another, all have been influenced by German, and none of the forms of speech in Scandinavian languages today can be regarded as Norn or Old Norse. All are significantly removed from their roots to the extent that speakers of the Scandinavian languages cannot easily read texts in Old Norse, and there is therefore a significant difference between on the one hand Danish, Norwegian and Swedish, and on the other Icelandic and Faroese.

The Viking language taken to the east has not survived. In Russia the descendants of the Vikings adopted Slavonic languages – though they made their impact in the very name Russia, meaning the land of the red-haired Vikings. A language, scant fragments of which were recorded in the Crimea in the eighteenth century and called by scholars Crimean Gothic, may in fact not be Gothic at all but a much altered form of the Norn language. It exists no longer.

Just as Icelandic, Faroese and especially Danish, Norwegian and Swedish are not Norn, so the language spoken in Orkney and Shetland was not Norn. The form 'Orkney and Shetland Norn' at least stresses that it is a product of Orkney and Shetland, though in many respects a new name would be preferable that excluded the word Norn: Orkney and Shetland Norn is a distinct language that developed in the islands.

The Vikings certainly brought their language to Orkney and Shetland. In the ninth century the islands spoke Norn. In the ninth and succeeding centuries they were part of a language and cultural community which spread over an enormous area of northern Europe and the north Atlantic. Norn was spoken throughout much of Scandinavia – certainly the coastal areas and the south, though in the fells of the northern interior and in the far north Norn gave way to various Saami (Lapp) languages. To the north and west Norn was spoken in the Faroe Islands and Iceland, and was subsequently to be carried by the Vikings to Greenland and America. In the south Norn was spoken in the south lands – the Scottish county of Sutherland, in Caithness, and in Ross and Cromarty. The Viking expansion into England resulted in Viking speakers on the whole of the English east coast. The Viking drive towards

Ireland took Norn to the Western Isles of Scotland, to the Isle of Man, to Ireland, and to the biggest city of the Viking world, Dublin. The eastern expansion of the Vikings created Norn-speaking communities in the heart of Russia, while Viking mercenaries were numerous in the Mediterranean, in Athens and Rome, and from the eleventh century played a leading role in the Crusades, taking Norn to Jerusalem and beyond. Even Baghdad and Tehran were visited by Vikings. The creation of a Viking stronghold in northern France – Normandy – placed the Vikings and their language at the heart of European politics. In early times Norn was the lingua franca of northern Europe and the North Atlantic, and an important language in eastern Europe, the Mediterranean and the Middle East. From the north shore of Norway to Sicily, from Jerusalem to Greenland and Newfoundland, Norn speakers could be found. Orkney and Shetland were at the crossroads of this great ethnic trading community.

We do have examples of the Viking language in Orkney and Shetland, for example from inscriptions in Orkney in the form of Viking graffiti on the inside of the ancient burial chamber of Maes Howe. A group of Icelandic Vikings returning from a crusade to Jerusalem in the 1150s decided to break into the ancient burial mound, perhaps in search of treasure, perhaps as a show of bravery. They left a series of inscriptions. One reads:

> Thessar runar reist sa mathr, er runstr er fyrin vestan haf, meth theiri oxi, er atti Gaukr Trandilssonr fyrir sunnan land.

This is good Norn, or indeed as the writer was from Iceland, good Old Icelandic. It presents no particular translation problems:

> These runes were carved by the best rune-master to the west of the ocean with the axe once owned by Gaukur Trandilsson who lived in the south [of Iceland].

We can also put it in a context, as the axe of Gaukur Trandilsson features in an Icelandic story, and his farmstead, buried in ash from an eruption of Mount Hekla, has recently been excavated. Orkney provides a fragment of language redolent with Viking history. Norn, Old Norse, Old Icelandic – the names are virtual synonyms – was certainly spoken on Orkney and Shetland.

In time the Viking Norn on Orkney and Shetland was replaced by Norwegian. The process was gradual, and much that is really Norwegian is called Norn. This new language was certainly spoken and written in Orkney and Shetland as first Norway then Denmark governed the islands. We have examples of very solid legal texts in Danish written in the islands by Danish rulers, and sometimes these Danish texts have misleadingly been called Norn texts, reflecting where they were written.

But Orkney and Shetland had something else, a home-grown development of the Viking language. Orkney and Shetland Norn is not Norn. It is similar to Norn, but different. The language was spoken throughout the islands, and may additionally have been spoken across the Pentland Firth in Caithness.

While something remains of Orkney and Shetland Norn, there is almost nothing of the Caithness Norn language. Most writers have assumed that it must have been similar to the Norn of Orkney and Shetland, though there is no reason why this should necessarily be so. The Viking settlement of Caithness seems to have been a little later than that in Orkney and Shetland, and the pre-existing linguistic framework was different, in that, for example, the Early English were presumably not in Caithness. It is possible – perhaps even likely – that Caithness Norn had significant differences from the Norn of Orkney and Shetland, and the Pentland Firth was enough of a barrier to preserve those differences. This book has little to say about Caithness Norn.

The idea that the Orkney and Shetland Norn was simply Norn has to be discounted. It is not tenable.

We know very little about the specific sounds of Orkney and Shetland Norn as represented by the chaotically spelled texts which have been preserved. Some commentators have seen in them what they assert to be evidence of a Scandinavian sound system, even specifically one from south-west Norway, the area that most of the Viking settlers of Orkney and Shetland came from. The materials in my view do not support such conclusions. Little more can be said about the sound system than that the sound -*th*- seems to be avoided, a feature continued today particularly in the English dialect of Shetland. This is a feature of Scandinavian languages, but it is also a feature of many forms of English, for example Irish English and some forms of London and Home Counties English. Around the world -*th*- is an exceptionally rare language sound, and while several languages have sounds which approximate to it (Spanish for example), among modern languages only English and Icelandic appear to use it. Both Old West Germanic and Old North Germanic had the sound, and it has been preserved in the standard form of one modern language from each group (English and Icelandic) and lost in others (for example, German and Dutch from the West group, the Scandinavian languages and Faroese from the East group.)

The grammar of Orkney and Shetland Norn has been considered to show many of the grammatical features of Old Norse. For example, it has been correctly pointed out that Orkney and Shetland Norn has two numbers (singular and plural), three genders (masculine, feminine and neuter), four cases (nominative, accusative, genitive and dative) and two main verb forms (present and past), all features characteristic of Old Norse. However, these features are also found in Old English. All that can really be said is that Orkney and Shetland Norn observes the grammatical characteristics common to Germanic languages.

The one grammatical feature of Orkney and Shetland Norn which does suggest a Norse affiliation is the use of suffixed definite articles. Old Norse, Old English and indeed all the old Germanic languages lack an article system comparable to that of modern English – that is to say they do not have equivalents for the definite article *the* and indefinite article *a*. While English (and German and Dutch) have developed *the* or its equivalent, the Scandinavian languages show a structure where the definite article is not usually a prefixed word but rather suffixed to the noun. Thus modern Norwegian has *hus* (house) and *huset* (the house). That Orkney and Shetland Norn uses this feature is probably best understood as a borrowing from Danish, the language of the ruling class in the Middle Ages. It was not a feature of the earliest forms of either Old English or Old Norse.

3.2 THE RECORDERS OF ORKNEY AND SHETLAND NORN

For the preservation of Orkney and Shetland Norn we are dependent on the work of two men about a hundred years apart: George Low and Jakob Jakobsen. Neither was a native of the islands, yet each had the interest to record what he found.

George Low (1747–95) was born in Forfarshire and came to Orkney as a minister. There his interests developed as a naturalist and local historian. He made just one visit to Shetland in what he termed his 'Grand Tour' of 1774, during which he visited most parts of Mainland and many of the islands, with Fair Isle being his only major miss. On a visit to Foula he found that Orkney and Shetland Norn was still remembered, and it was here that he recorded material including the longest extant text in the language, *The Ballad of Hildina*. His transcription of this song remembered by an elderly informant is particularly remarkable as George Low was not a linguist, and had no knowledge either of an Old Germanic language, or any modern languages save English and French. He was without the training in methodology for such a task which today is considered an essential foundation for recording an oral language.

The notes of his 1774 trip were not published in his lifetime, but preserved as a manuscript and published more than a century later as *A Tour through the Islands of Orkney and Schetland* (Kirkwall, 1879). George Low's work reflects a lively curiosity about everything to do with Orkney and Shetland, from pictures of monuments to descriptions of ancient artefacts which had been dug up. Without his manuscript – now in the Advocate's Library, Edinburgh – we would have but the scantiest material for Orkney and Shetland Norn.

A century later what he regarded as the Norn language of Shetland – not Orkney – was recorded by Jakob Jakobsen (1864–1918), the major figure in Faroese philology, and an important contributor to the historic study of the Germanic languages. Within the Faroe Islands he is rightly regarded as the father of the modern Faroese language, for without his efforts the language would most probably have died. He is also recognised as a leading folklorist and preserver of stories and verses primarily from the Faroe Islands, and has been commemorated there, for example, by a postage stamp in his honour (1980). Born in the Faroe Islands, he was educated in Denmark and Scotland. His philological interests led him to Shetland, and what he saw as the Norn language of Shetland is set out in three substantial books (in Danish): an 1897 study of Shetland Norn, a 1901 commentary on the place-names of Shetland, and published from 1908 to 1912 his massive *Etymologisk Ordbog*, in which he sets out the distinctive vocabulary of the English dialect he found spoken on Shetland.

Jakobsen was a philologist working within the so-called neo-grammarian tradition. Starting in German universities in the late 1880s and 1890s – particularly the Humboldt in Berlin and the Leopoldian in Breslau (now Wroclaw) – the neo-grammarians lifted philology from an antiquarian pursuit to a science governed by rules by setting out changes within languages which conform to precisely formulated rules. Jakobsen applied these ideas to Old Norse/Icelandic and to the language of the Faroe Islands, and produced material which is of seminal importance, standing at the forefront of the academic study of the history of the Scandinavian languages. Any modern account of these languages will refer to him. His reputation and influence have meant that his mark has been set also on the study of Orkney and Shetland Norn. While more than a century of scholars have developed and modified his views on the history of the Scandinavian languages, very few have reassessed his work on Orkney and Shetland Norn. Such a reassessment is needed. In particular there are two underlying assumptions in his work, both questionable:

- the idea that Orkney and Shetland Norn is no more than a dialect of Old Norse, when in fact it is a unique language which developed on the islands;
- the idea that the modern dialect of Shetland is some form of fusion – in today's terminology a creole – of English and Norn – which it simply is not.

Additionally there are mistakes within his work, including much of his collection of presumed Norn vocabulary from the English-spoken dialect of Shetland. These cautions noted, there can be no doubt that our debt to Jakobsen is substantial. His untiring industry has left a considerable volume of material for posterity to work on.

Yet while we recognise his achievement, Jakobsen's work must nonetheless be approached with considerable care. There are two sorts of problems. First of all, he wanted to find Old Norse in Shetland, and there is always a risk that a researcher's work will be compromised when they wish to reach a particular conclusion. Second, there is the virtual impossibility of some of his findings. He lists an amazing number of distinct Shetland words which he believed he had identified – about 10,000. No dialect of any language ever has been shown to have this sort of number of unique forms. Very few speakers of any language use more than half this number of words in the totality of their spoken language, and to assert that 10,000 distinct dialect words were in use alongside the whole standard English vocabulary must be wrong.

That said, there is no doubt that Shetland had a rich dialect – just not as rich as Jakobsen suggested. Jakobsen has preserved much of the Shetland dialect that would otherwise have been lost, along with a few howlers that I see as coming from the Jakobsen problem of being too keen to identify new words. An example of what I choose to regard as the Jakobsen problem is the word 'drat-sie' as a Shetland word for otter. I suppose the possibility exists that 'dratsie' really was an old Shetland dialect word for otter – I cannot totally exclude this possibility. But this is most unlikely. Consider the words used for otter in other Germanic languages. In Anglo-Saxon it is *otor*, in Old Norse *otr*, in Danish *odder*, in Swedish *utter*, in Dutch *otter*. Even looking further afield there are cognate forms in languages including Russian, Lithuanian and Greek. It is most implausible that Shetland had the strange form 'dratsie' as a dialect word for 'otter'.

Of course Shetland today does have 'dratsie' as just such a dia-lect word. It is heavily promoted by the Shetland Tourist Office publications as an example of distinct Shetland dialect. There are certainly people today who use the word 'dratsie' to refer to an otter, and it is likely that it was used by some in Shetland since the publication of Jakobsen's dictionary as a deliberate adoption of what was believed to be a traditional form, so the word has now been in use for as long as living memory goes. In this restricted sense, it is today a dialect word in Shetland. But that it existed before Jakobsen is most unlikely.

A plausible explanation for *dratsie* can be advanced. Philol-ogists of Jakobsen's day had a practical method of establishing dialect words from informants, a technique still used today. The researcher simply shows the informant a picture of something and asks them what they call it. Presumably Jakobsen showed his informants a picture of an otter – probably a very small black and white line drawing with many other animals on that page – and asked his informants what they called the animal. Otters are now making a comeback in Shetland and can today be seen without too much difficulty. However in Jakobsen's day otters were not found in most parts of Shetland, and most Shetlanders would therefore never have seen one. Confronted with Jakobsen's small picture and the question 'What do you call this?' the possible answers were:

- the informant correctly identified an otter and called it an otter;
- the informant was unable to identify the animal and said they did not recognise it;
- the informant misidentified the animal.

Plausibly, one of Jakobsen's informants produced the third option. Given the poor quality of the pictures typically used in Jakobsen's day, and – who knows – maybe also poor eyesight on the part of his informant, there is no surprise that misidentifications should have happened. *Dratsie* can reasonably be analysed as the well-recorded Shetland definite article *da* and *ratsie*, a well-known Scots diminutive form for *rat*.

I cannot totally exclude the possibility that *dratsie* really is a genuine, old Shetland form for otter, and I know that it has now become a Shetland word for otter, but the balance of probability is that one informant mistook the picture of an otter shown and called it a rat, and that was enough to get the word into Jakobsen's dictionary.

Jakobsen is a great philologist and the seminal figure in the study of the old Scandinavian languages. Nevertheless, my inclination is to regard Jakobsen with great caution, and particularly to take care in dealing with his interpretations of Orkney and Shetland Norn. More than a hundred years later, approaches and techniques have developed, and we can realise the weaknesses in his work while appreciating its strengths.

3.3 SIMILARITIES WITH OLD NORSE AND OLD ENGLISH

The relationship of Orkney and Shetland Norn to Old Norse and Old English may be explored through an examination of texts of the Lord's Prayer in these three languages. I have used below a version collected in Orkney and believed to be the more conservative of the two preserved – alongside the Lord's Prayer in Old Norse and Old English.

First in Orkney and Shetland Norn:

Favor i ir i chimrie,
Helleur ir i nam thite,
gilla cosdum thite cumma,
veya thine mota vara gort
o yurn sinna gort i chimrie,
ga vus da on da dalight brow vora
Firgive vus sinna vora
sin vee Firgive sindara mutha vus,
lyv vus ye i tumtation,
min delivera vus fro olt ilt,
Amen.

The Old Norse version (with orthography modified to our alphabet) reads:

Father vár es ert í himenríki,
verthi nafn thitt hæilagt
Til kome ríke thitt,
værthi vili thin
sva a iarthu sem í himnum.
Gef oss í dag brauth vort dagligt
Ok fyr gefthu oss synther órar,
sem vér fyr gefom theim er vith oss hafa misgert
Leithd oss eigi í freistni,
heldr leys thv oss frá öllu illu,
Amen.

There are significant differences here. Certainly, from the impression of a casual comparison, Orkney and Shetland Norn cannot be regarded simply as a form of Old Norse.

Similarly, the comparison may be made with the Lord's Prayer in Old English. Again modifying the spelling for our orthography, this reads:

Faether ūre, thū the eart on heofonum;
Sī thīn nāma gehālgod,
tō becume thīn rīce,
gewurthe thīn willa,
on eorthan swā swā on heofonum.
ūrne gedaeghwamlican hlāf syle ūs tōdaeg,
and forgyf ūs ūre gyltas,
swā swā wē forgyfath ūrum gyltendum,
and ne gelaed thū ūs on costnunge,
ac ālys ūs of yfele, sōthlīce,
Amen.

Comparing the significant words of the three versions highlights
the similarities and differences:

Orkney & Shetland Norn	Old Norse	Old English
Favor	Father	Faether
Chimrie	Himenriki	Heofonum
Helleur	Hæilagt	geHalgod
Nam	Nafn	Nama
Cosdum	Rike	Rice
Mota	Vili	Willa
Yurn	Iarthu	Eorthan
Ga	Gef	Syle
Da	Dag	Todaeg
Dalight	Dagligt	Gedaeghwamlican
Firgive	Fyr gefthu	Forgyf
Sinna	Synther	Gyltas
Lyv	Leith	geLaed
Tumtation	Freistni	Costnunge
Delivera	Leys	aLys
Ilt	Illu	Yfele

Of these sixteen words, most have an etymological relationship between all the three languages. To say that an Orkney and Shetland Norn word is closer to Old Norse or to Old English is ultimately a matter of judgement. On my count however:

5 words are closest to Old Norse	*Chimrie, ga, dalight, sinna, ilt*
2 words are closest to Old English	*Nam, yurn*
5 words are equally close to both Old Norse and Old English	*Favour, helleur, da, firgive, lyv*
4 words are not close to either	*Cosdum, mota, tumtation, delivera*

Different versions of the Lord's Prayer from the three languages would give modified results. However some key issues are as follows:

- Orkney and Shetland Norn is significantly removed from both Old Norse and Old English. It certainly is not just a form of Old Norse.
- Many of the words used are common to both Old Norse and Old English, and could be shown as a development of either language.
- On this tiny sample there are more words from Old Norse than Old English. However the Old English *gedaeghwamlican* is a form quickly abandoned in English versions of the Lord's Prayer – its length reflects its linguistic awkwardness. Similarly Old English *syle* was replaced by an alternative root which yields our form *give*. The Old English version of the Lord's Prayer is older than the Old Norse version, a feature which distorts a comparison such as this. Arguably the Orkney and Shetland Norn version is actually closer to Old English than this simple comparison suggests.
- Orkney and Shetland Norn is not simply following either language. It is its own language.

3.4 How Language Changes Work

All languages undergo changes through time. For a twenty-first-century speaker of Modern English even the English of Shakespeare and the King James Bible can seem old fashioned, though these forms from the late sixteenth and early seventeenth century are still regarded by linguists as Modern English. Further back is the form of English called Middle English, best known to readers today from the writings of Geoffrey Chaucer, which while still comprehensible by an educated native speaker has significant differences.

Changes can be at all levels of a language. The most far-reaching are at the level of syntax, the fundamental traffic-rules by which a language operates and orders its words. Changes in syntax are usually equated with changes in the very nature of a language, in that it is because the syntax has changed that we begin to consider that a new language has developed. Such changes are the rarest sorts of change.

Changes in grammar can also happen. At their simplest these changes mean that a particular grammatical form changes to another form. Within English we see such changes, for example, in the development of Middle English to Modern English. So in Modern English we have a very large category of phrasal verbs, forms like *to go in, to go out, to go up, to go down, to go under.* All these can be replaced by a single-word verb: *to enter, to leave, to ascend, to descend, to sink.* But the phrasal verb forms, often verb plus preposition, are extremely common in Modern English, and it is unthinkable to hold a conversation without using them. In Chaucer phrasal verbs are only rarely found, while in earlier Middle English texts there are no phrasal verbs at all, and there are none in Old English. The growth of a system of phrasal verbs is a fundamental development which makes Modern English different from Middle English. It is a big change, and grammatical changes such as this are not particularly common.

Languages also change in their vocabulary. In English today this is a big area of change as new words appear to handle new concepts of modern living. All languages, all the time, change their vocabulary, sometimes quickly and sometimes slowly. The results are highly visible, and speakers of a language will be acutely aware of differences in vocabulary used by speakers of their language from a different locality, or by a different social class, or by a different generation.

Today many and varied changes in English are taking place, with the result that the language is experiencing a period of rapid change. New vocabulary is entering the language at the fastest rate ever, while the global spread of English is creating a multiplicity of English styles. Change is happening, and we are all aware of it. There is nothing unusual about this.

Fast or slow, changes in the language have always taken place. In our time the change is primarily in the area of vocabulary. In the Germanic languages a particularly rapid period of change occurred in the second half of the fifth century, roughly AD 450–500. This was not primarily a vocabulary change, but rather a fundamental change in the sound of the language, with a series of related changes taking place in vowels. As a consequence words were modified with syllables lost, and the confusion caused prompted secondary changes in grammar and vocabulary. This is a fundamental feature of all Germanic languages, and can be seen in both west and north groups, and in all the extant modern languages, including English, German, Dutch, Icelandic, Faroese, Danish, Norwegian and Swedish.

All these languages undergo a major change in their sounds in the early fifth century called *i*-mutation (this is explained below, section 3.5). Germanic languages before this time (Gothic, some early Scandinavian runic inscriptions) don't show *i*-mutation at all. Afterwards they all show *i*-mutation – with the one exception of the Orkney and Shetland Norn. Curiously, this language shows occasional examples of *i*-mutation, but not the regular pattern of all other Germanic languages. This is truly remarkable, as there should not be an exception. The whole principle of comparative philology is that absolute rules can be established which permit of no exceptions. The rule we have is that the Germanic languages all experienced a particular sound change at a particular time, and we should not need to say 'all, but with one exception'.

The only way philologists can explain the observed position is through the concept of a language isolate – a language geographically detached from all others in the group at the key time. Purely from a linguistic perspective this would suggest that a population speaking a Germanic language (the ancestor of Orkney and Shetland Norn) moved to an isolated area before the early fifth century, remained there, and at a later time came into contact with another Germanic population.

When I first thought about this I formed the hypothesis that a few Norsemen reached Orkney and Shetland before the early fifth century, but that the main period of Norse settlement was much later, the familiar Viking migration from AD 790. With this hypothesis it is necessary to assume some sort of disruption of trans-North Sea links around the time when the change took place, and it is hard to see what could have caused such a disruption.

However, historical evidence suggests that the settlers were the Early English, not Norse. The hypothesis, therefore, is that a group of Early English reached Orkney and Shetland before the time of *i*-mutation, were isolated from other Germanic speakers at the time when the mutation took place, and continued to speak a form of Germanic which does not show *i*-mutation. The Old English they spoke was very heavily influenced by Old Norse, to the extent that the vocabulary used is largely Old Norse, along with some of the grammar and many of the set expressions.

3.5 *i*-MUTATION IN THE GERMANIC LANGUAGES

Changes in the pronunciation of a language do not take place at an even speed. For example, there have been changes in the way in which British English today is pronounced compared to a century ago, but these changes are actually rather small. English today sounds much as it did in the early years of the twentieth century. Even going back another century or two we do not find major changes. If we look back as far as Shakespeare, some pronunciation changes are apparent, enough for Shakespeare performed with an original accent to seem strange to our ear. Yet, notwithstanding these differences, the sounds of Shakespeare's English are still fundamentally those of the language we speak today.

Such modest change in pronunciation is the usual state of languages for hundreds of years. However, there are other more dramatic changes which can happen, and which transform the sounds of a language in a generation or two. No one who speaks English today has personal experience of such a change. One past dramatic sound change was as English moved from Old English to Middle English. This transition is conventionally dated as the 150 years from 1100 to 1250, though it happened earlier in some dialects of English than in others, so in each area the change took place within a couple of generations, say sixty years. During this time a change occurred for every single diphthong in the language. Every diphthong was lost, and replaced by a monophthong. Thus for example the Old English word for cheese, *chiese*, had its diphthong -*ie*- replaced by the long vowel -*ee*-, giving the word we know today.

The motivation for such a dramatic change in sounds is not particularly clear. To an extent it can be seen as a reflection of phonological laziness. It takes a little more energy for the tongue to form a diphthong than a single vowel, so in the interests of less work a single vowel makes sense. This explanation is not really satisfactory, though it is the only one we have. The loss of diphthongs caused all sorts of confusion in meaning, which would seem to be a very good reason for retaining them. It would have caused difficulties of understanding between different generations, and as the change happened at slightly different times in different dialects it would have caused confusion between speakers of different dialects. A further absurdity of the change is that almost as soon as the diphthongs were lost, a second process created diphthongs in some words that had previously had monophthongs.

The reality is that we are guessing at a reason why all diphthongs were lost as we move from Old English to Middle English. What we do know is when the process happened, and that it happened 100 per cent of the time, no exceptions. The change must have been strange indeed for people who lived through it.

It has been suggested that in today's English the sound -*th*- is a candidate for similar rapid change. Very few languages around the world have a -*th*- sound (English and Icelandic are sometimes claimed to be the only two), and this is because -*th*- is rather difficult to pronounce. Native speakers are used to it, but second language speakers struggle, often even the most proficient. The argument is that today with so many non-native speakers of English struggling with the -*th*- sound, it is set to change into something else, perhaps -*t*- or -*f*-, and this change might be as sudden as the loss of Old English diphthongs. The possibility exists, though prediction of language change by historical linguists seems to be an exceptionally imprecise discipline.

In the early period of the development of the Germanic languages a change in the pronunciation of the languages took place. While comparable to the monophthongisation of Old English diphthongs or the putative loss of -*th*- in that it took place suddenly throughout the language, it differs in that it is more complex.

The process is usually called *i*-mutation – though it can also be called *i*-umlaut, *j*-mutation or front mutation. The process concerns the position adopted by the tip of the tongue when vowel sounds are formed. The English words *cart*, *cot* and *cut* all have vowel sounds which are formed with the tip of the tongue towards the back of the mouth. By contrast *cat*, *ket* (in kettle) and *kit* all have vowel sounds formed with the tip of the tongue towards the front of the mouth. It is perfectly possible to think about the position of your tongue as you say these vowels and become aware of where the tongue is. It is also possible to distinguish between vowels which are formed towards the bottom of the mouth: *cart* and *cat*; towards the middle of the mouth, *cot* and *ket*, and towards the top of the mouth, *cut* and *kit*. In these examples the consonants stay the same (the variation between *c* and *k* is purely a spelling convention) and the different words are created by the different tongue-tip position as the vowels are made. Six basic positions are therefore possible for stressed vowels.

The sound change that occurred in Germanic is a movement of vowels towards the *i*-vowel. Take, for example, a Germanic word **goos* (the * means it is a reconstructed form as we have no written records). In fact **goos* both means and was pronounced as Modern English *goose*. However, Germanic languages did not form plurals by adding an -*s*; rather, they usually used a final -*n*, and often had to insert a vowel or vowels between the stem and the -*n*. The plural of **goos* was **goosian*. The word **goosian* is perfectly straightforward to pronounce, but it does exercise the tongue. The long vowel -*oo*- is middle back, while the vowel -*i*- is top front, quite a distance apart. The change which occurred is set out in terms of laziness – rather than make this abrupt transition in terms of tongue tip position, people started anticipating the -*i*- by forming the earlier vowel in a different way. Vowels which were followed by -*i*- were moved a step closer to -*i*-. Here a back vowel -*oo*- is moved to the equivalent front vowel -*ee*-, and a new plural form created as **geesian*. This form would have made sense, but suddenly the ending -*ian* has become redundant. The plural sense is conveyed by the change of vowel alone, so a new plural form emerges as **gees*. This particular vocabulary item has been unchanged for around 1,500 years, so today we say one goose but two geese.

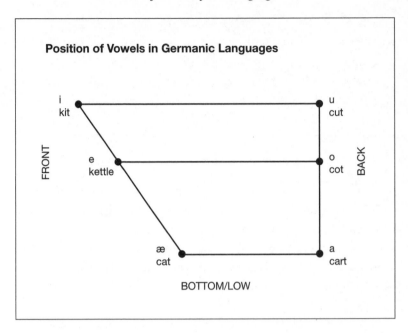

Position of Vowels in Germanic Languages

Examples of the effects of *i*-mutation abound in the English language today, as well as in the Scandinavian languages and in German. For example:

u>i
full, fill
mouse, mice
louse, lice

o>e
goose, geese
foot, feet
tooth, teeth
old, elder
long, length
strong, strength
food, feed

a>æ
latter, late

æ>e
sat, set
Angle, English

e>i
sheep, sheep

a>e (before a nasal)
man, men

The phenomenon of *i*-mutation is a key factor affecting the form of all medieval and modern Germanic languages. It happened in all, and it is entrenched in all because many of the changes are grammatical. The changes cannot be reversed. It is unthinkable to imagine English – or any other Germanic language – without these changes.

The process called *i*-mutation is not strictly unique to the Germanic languages. It has been seen by some linguists in Portuguese as an explanation for changing vowels in the verb to do (*fiz*, I did; *fez*, he did). Something similar may have happened in the Celtic languages. Nor is it unique to Indo-European languages, for there is a comparable process in Japanese and in Hebrew, representatives of two completely dissimilar groups. Nevertheless, it is the Germanic languages that show the full impact of this remarkable change.

While the motivation for such a traumatic change is unclear, it can be dated with reasonable certainty. It is a process which fits neatly into the second half of the fifth century. There is no sign of *i*-mutation before around AD 450, while by 500 the process is complete everywhere. It took place a little earlier in Anglo-Saxon and Old Norse than in Old High German. Half a century is in linguistic terms a very fast change indeed. The reality of a change at this speed is that children used different forms to their parents, and the change would therefore have been apparent to people living at the time who would have heard it happen in the course of their lifetime.

Philologists have written extensively on the process of *i*-mutation, frequently in exhaustive detail, but few have set out in a few sentences just how remarkable it is. It is remarkable first of all because the process occurred over a wide area. This suggests substantial interaction between communities over a wide geographic area – indeed, there seems to be no possible explanation for this other than substantial interaction. Presumably this interaction would be realised through many and frequent migrations of individuals, families and whole communities in what was an age of migration, as well as through trading contacts. Then the process is remarkable because it happened within what scholars today tend to regard as three distinct languages: Old English, Old Norse and Old High German, as well as in half a dozen less well recorded Germanic languages. In reality the very fact that the process took place over these 'languages' demonstrates a high degree of mutual comprehension between these forms of speech. In the fifth century we have to regard them not as separate languages, but rather as one language marked by dialects and with few difficulties in communication between speakers of different dialects.

i-mutation happened everywhere in the Germanic world. Traditionally the one footnote to this statement is that we do not see it in Gothic because the Gothic texts that are preserved pre-date this fifth-century change. But we do see it in absolutely every other Germanic language.

Every language, that is, except Orkney and Shetland Norn. Uniquely, we have one Germanic language which post-dates the change, but which fails to show this ubiquitous phenomenon.

3.6 The Absence of *i*-Mutation in Orkney and Shetland Norn

There are no comfortable explanations for why a universal of all Germanic languages is missing in Orkney and Shetland Norn. But missing it is. The feature simply is not present in the language. There are a few occasions when different processes have produced something which looks similar to *i*-mutation, but this is not *i*-mutation.

An example from Orkney and Shetland Norn is *Jarlin*, the Earl, the hero of *The Ballad of Hildina*. This form quite simply should not exist. It should be **Jerl-*, which modified to the conventions of our spelling system is the familiar *Earl*. Similarly *yamna* (meaning 'always') should be **yemna*, and even the name *Yalts* (Shetlanders) should be **Yelts*. Examples are legion; *i*-mutation did not happen.

It cannot be that *i*-mutation was lost, for as an irreversible one-way process it can never be lost. Once the syllables containing the -*i*- vowel have been lost, the phonological environment becomes identical to other vowels, so there is nothing to prompt a change. There are indeed processes which can move vowel sounds in the other direction to *i*-mutation. These back mutations, particularly one called *u*-mutation, are a feature of many languages. However these mutations affect all vowels equally. Their influence is not restricted to those that have previously undergone *i*-mutation. Back mutation cannot be an explanation.

Philology also has the concept of analogy, where forms in a language will be influenced by those of another language it comes into contact with. Had Orkney and Shetland Norn somehow come into contact with a Germanic language that had not undergone *i*-mutation, analogy could possibly explain the situation observed. But of course this did not happen, for there was no un-mutated Germanic language. Indeed, there is some truth in the converse – the impact of Old Norse on Orkney and Shetland Norn was to introduce the occasional vowel which resembles an *i*-mutation.

There is only one possible philological explanation for the situation observed. This is that at the time when *i*-mutation took place in all the other Germanic languages, Orkney and Shetland Norn was an isolate, a language cut off from other forms of the early Germanic languages. If we knew nothing of the settlement history of Orkney and Shetland and were working only from the evidence of language, we would confidently assert that a Germanic people settled prior to *circa* AD 450, and were isolated from other Germanic speakers at least for the fifty years roughly 450–500, say two generations.

This is not in keeping with the received view of Viking settlement from AD 790 as the first Germanic migration to the islands. Logically there are three possible explanations:

1. The received story of settlement by the Vikings is correct, but they came from an isolated community somewhere in Norway, so that it is in Norway that the *i*-mutation failed.
2. The Vikings – or their ancestors from Norway – arrived much earlier, at least prior to AD 450, and therefore more than three centuries before it is usually claimed they arrived.
3. The Early English arrived prior to 450.

While the first explanation is logically sound, it fails on two practical grounds. First, an environment in Norway where an isolated community may have been established simply does not exist. Settlement of Norway was limited to the coastal margins, while the mountains and fjords discouraged land transport. Travel was by sea, and every community was joined to every other by the sea. There were no isolates within Norway. Then to make this explanation work it is necessary to assume that the Viking migration to Orkney and Shetland was from one isolated community and that community alone, and that the migrations via Orkney and Shetland to the Faroe Islands, Iceland and beyond were from other communities entirely. As it happens, we do know that south-west Norway was the home of many (but not all) of the Viking settlers of Orkney and Shetland (and the Faroe Islands and Iceland), and by no stretch of the imagination could this part of Norway be considered isolated. The first logical possibility simply is not tenable.

It is plausible that the ancestors of the Vikings crossed from Norway much earlier than is generally suggested. The early Norse certainly had ships, and while they were not suited for open seas there is no absolute reason why they should not have made the journey. Probably some did.

The third possibility best explains the evidence we have. We know the Early English were making many voyages across the North Sea at this time, and there is no obstacle to their having extended their voyages to Orkney and Shetland – indeed, we know they were there. The whole voyage can be made without losing sight of land, and is therefore likely to have been more frequent than voyages from Norway at this time. There are early historians who place the English in the islands at the appropriate time. Furthermore, the massive disruption in the fifth century as the Roman Empire failed gives an environment in which the English in Orkney and Shetland could become isolated for a period, including the key years when *i*-mutation took place.

3.7 THE CREATION OF ORKNEY AND SHETLAND NORN

The historical materials discussed above, along with the linguistic evidence presented, prompts revision of the established history of Orkney and Shetland Norn. The first Germanic language in Orkney and Shetland was not the Viking language but rather the language spoken by the Early English settlers. Exactly when they arrived is not indicated either by a historical source or by features within the language, but the early fourth century AD seems most likely. This is around the date of Early English incursions on the Saxon Shore, around the time of the Saxon trading settlement down-river from London, and around the time when there were numerous incursions on the whole east coast of England. It is part of a larger phenomenon than a migration to Orkney and Shetland alone. The language found in the islands at this time and spoken by the Early English is the direct ancestor of Modern English – and Modern Lowland Scots – and not of the Scandinavian languages. At this early date the differences between the language which became English and that which became the Scandinavian languages were tiny. They were differences in dialect rather than language, and mutually comprehensible one with the other.

Quite how the Early English and the Celtic-speaking Picts lived alongside one another is a matter for conjecture. In linguistic terms there are three possible models:

- Political unity within each of the island groups might not have been maintained, so that some islands may have been taken over entirely by the Early English and the Pictish–Celtic and Early English communities lived separately.
- Orkney and Shetland may have been multicultural societies with several migrant populations living within a Pictish–Celtic mainstream. Thus the Early English preserved their language in much the same way that the Jews of Europe preserved their language despite living among a host community.
- The Early English may have entered the islands as a ruling class, and imposed their language on the majority population. This is the model by which, for example, the English language was brought to the Indian subcontinent.

There is little evidence to test these models. Rather, we can advance conjectures based on probability. The first model, which sees the Early English in effect taking over a few islands, seems inherently implausible, and as far as I am aware the archaeological record does not hint at differing cultures on different islands at this period. Probably this model can be set aside. The second model, multiculturalism, has some points in its favour. The islands certainly were open to many cultural influences at this time. Yet the circumstances which preserve languages within a host community are most often encountered in urban societies. For example, the Yiddish language in Europe was largely a feature of the cities, and goes hand in hand with the establishment of ghettos. While Yiddish was spoken in certain rural areas, it is doubtful that it would have survived if it had existed in these areas alone. This second model is certainly possible, but would be surprising if it is true – which leaves model number three. The 'ruling class' phenomenon is very common indeed in language spread. The scenario is that a small group of migrants or invaders are able to establish themselves as the rulers – usually through superior social structures rather than through superior force. The language of the rulers spreads downwards to the ruled, so that within a few generations the whole population has switched to the language of the ruling class. We are increasingly realising that this is the model by which English was brought to England, as the majority population in England remained the peoples indigenous at the time of the end of Roman rule. As this is the linguistic development in England, there is reason to think that a comparable development may be found in other lands to which the English migrated. The balance of probabilities is in favour of this third model. Some scant support for this model can be obtained from the concept of Orkney and Shetland as semi-detached from Pictish Scotland at this time. They are not one of the key, named, Pictish kingdoms, though they are certainly within the Pictish sphere of influence.

Following migration from the European continent the Early English community must have maintained a degree of separation from other Germanic-speakers at least through the crucial period when i-mutation was taking place. The collapse of order as the Roman Empire broke up provides an environment of disruption in which it is possible to envisage a group of people largely cut off from other speakers of their language.

My personal view is that on the eve of the Viking invasion the population of Orkney and Shetland, though ethnically Pictish and culturally influenced by Celtic contacts, had given up both Pictish and Celtic languages and were already speaking a Germanic language, Early English. This state of affairs goes a long way to explain the rarity of non-Germanic place-names in Orkney and Shetland.

In terms of language and culture – though not ethnicity – the people of Orkney and Shetland were very close indeed to the Viking invaders. This is why neither history nor archaeology can find any record of the coming of the Vikings. It was not quite that the Vikings were already there, but rather that their very close cousins the Early English were there, and in linguistic and cultural terms were already dominating the islands. There is no great change in either language or culture associated with the Viking age. Rather the Viking age establishes the islands as a trading crossroads, and encourages links with countries to which the trade routes led. Thus in the Viking age links are strengthened to the Viking north of Scotland, to Ireland, to the Faroe Islands and Iceland, and especially to Norway. They are weakened to Gaelic-speaking Scotland, and to England. The situation is right for modification of the language towards the Viking way of speech, and this indeed happened.

The Viking impact was of course significant, but in ways different from those usually assumed. It was not an invasion by an alien and hostile people, rather a migration by people very much like those already living in the islands. In linguistic terms two distinct strands can be seen. One is the use first of Old Norse and later of Norwegian and Danish by the rulers of the islands, so that we do see, for example, documents in perfectly good Danish written in the islands. The other is the development of the Early English language under the influence of Old Norse. Much Old Norse vocabulary and even grammar came into Orkney and Shetland English, but the English roots survived – particularly the vowels without *i*-mutation – along with the indigenous population which included an Early English strand. The language that emerged towards the end of the Viking age was greatly influenced by the Viking language – but crucially was not that language. Rather it was a home-grown island product, and therefore a unique, independent language. For centuries it was the mother tongue of Orcadians and Shetlanders, the language particularly suited to express the ideas of their culture and environment. It was – and remains – an integral part of the heritage of the islands.

3.8 The Death of Orkney and Shetland Norn

The decline and ultimate death of Orkney and Shetland Norn is part of a widespread, worldwide process of language extinction in the face of encroachment by English and other (mainly European) languages. Today around the world languages are dying out at the fastest rate ever, many completely unrecorded or with just the sort of sketchy recording that we have for Orkney and Shetland Norn. Of the indigenous languages of the British Isles that survived into the modern age, all except English have undergone a substantial decline. Welsh is the strongest survivor, and along with Irish and Scots Gaelic is at least as secure as any minority language can ever be. By contrast, Romany and Shelta, the languages of British gypsies and travellers, are now declining rapidly in the British Isles. Manx and Cornish, like Orkney and Shetland Norn, have become extinct, though both have revival movements. Orkney and Shetland Norn and Cornish, languages spoken at opposite extremities of the British Isles, declined and became extinct at much the same time and for similar reasons, though while Orkney and Shetland Norn died almost unnoticed, the process of the death of Cornish was observed by commentators of the time and gives some insights into the demise of Orkney and Shetland Norn.

The decline of Orkney and Shetland Norn began around 1400 and was rapid, and it is unlikely that the language outlived the eighteenth century as a means of everyday communication, though some very restricted usage continued through much of the nineteenth century and possibly even later.

At the beginning of the fifteenth century, Orkney and Shetland Norn was the predominant language of Orkney and Shetland, but competing with other languages. The four principal languages of Orkney and Shetland were:

1. Orkney and Shetland Norn. The language of most of the indigenous population of Orkney and Shetland. The language was a spoken vernacular only, and not written down.
2. Old Norse and its descendant languages. The Norwegians appointed a ruling class to govern Orkney and Shetland who were Norwegian and whose language was a development of Old Norse. Similar though Orkney and Shetland Norn and Old

Norse were, they were by no means identical and it is important
to maintain the distinction. Old Norse – or Norwegian, or Danish – as used in Orkney and Shetland was a written as well as a
spoken language of the ruling elite, and documents do survive
written in the language in the islands.

3. Scots Gaelic. This Celtic language has a long history on Orkney
   and Shetland, being the language of one of the earliest groups
   of settlers. It declined from the late eighth century and had presumably become extinct as an indigenous language well before
   the beginning of the fifteenth century. However, the proximity
   of Gaelic-speaking Scotland and the enduring missionary zeal of
   Celtic Christianity ensured Scots Gaelic the place of first foreign
   language. In interaction with Scotland the people of Orkney and
   Shetland needed this language.

4. Merchants from beyond Scotland brought their own languages,
   mostly Germanic. Old Norse dialects were well represented.
   Norwegian, Danish, Faroese and Icelandic merchants all spoke
   Old Norse-descended dialects, as did merchants from Scotland's
   Western Isles. From the southern shore of the North Sea came
   the related language of Dutch or Low German. English traders brought their language, and as English became increasingly
   adopted in Scotland the Scots also imported English.

This range of languages put Orkney and Shetland Norn under
strain. Nor did the language have particular strengths that would have
ensured its survival. Writing was seen as something which took place
in other languages. The prestige languages of church and government
were first Norwegian, later Danish, and later still English. There was
no overseas community that spoke the language to give it strength
– specifically, the next archipelago, the Faroe Islands, did not speak
the same language. Late in the history of the islands, as English took
over from Danish as the language of prestige, it is just about possible
that first-language English-speakers used a few words of Orkney and
Shetland Norn to communicate with Danes and Norwegians. One of
the last informants of the language on Foula is reported as calling it
Danish, which probably hints at its use in this context.

For speakers of a language with the vibrancy and international spread of English, the very idea of language death can be hard to comprehend. Models with which we are most familiar are unhelpful. We think of Latin as a dead language, while in fact Latin didn't die, but changed progressively into other languages living today, including Italian, Spanish and French. Ancient Greek similarly gave way to Modern Greek. In the death of Orkney and Shetland Norn we are by contrast seeing the passing away of a form of speech and the cultural heritage embodied in a mother tongue without leaving a successor.

Language death has been particularly common in the twentieth century, and seems likely to be even more prevalent in the twenty-first. For example, at the start of the twentieth century there were around 1,000 indigenous languages spoken within Brazil; by the end of the century the number was just 200. Improved communications go hand in hand with a reduction in the number of languages. What happened to Orkney and Shetland Norn is part of a worldwide phenomenon.

Quite when a language can be said to be dead is a matter for debate. In the case of the Cornish language a curiously precise date is conventionally given for the death of the language. In the churchyard of Paul, Cornwall is a monument to a woman from the neighbouring fishing hamlet of Mousehole, which reads:

> Here lieth interred Dorothy Pentreath who died in 1777. Said to have been the last person who conversed in the ancient Cornish, the peculiar language of this county from the earliest records till it expired in the eighteenth century in this parish of Saint Paul.

The inscription raises a host of questions. If Dorothy Pentreath was the last speaker of Cornish, who was she speaking to? The answer usually given is to several women of her generation who understood Cornish but could not speak it – and who it seems were speaking to her in English. Was she truly a mother-tongue speaker of Cornish? It seems her peers were bilingual but favoured English, that being their mother tongue. And was she really the last speaker? Even the grave inscription implies doubt, reporting instead a tradition. No doubt there were other people in Cornwall about this time who had some knowledge of the language, and may even have had the language as their mother tongue. Recently we have discovered that languages can effectively hide, even in the British Isles, as speakers choose not to let outsiders know they speak what they regard as a low-prestige language. This is particularly prevalent if the language is regarded as being of low status and therefore somehow shameful, or if it becomes a 'secret' language by which a group assert their identity. The outstanding British example is Shelta, a Celtic language once thought to be all but extinct, but now accepted as having some thousands of speakers. Just because outsiders seeking to record Orkney and Shetland Norn could find no speakers we cannot conclude that the language was truly dead.

All these reservations aside, 1777 is a convenient date to accept for the death of Cornish. The death of Orkney and Shetland Norn cannot be set with similar precision, though it was around this time.

Its last survival was on Foula, today one of the three remotest communities in the British Isles. Tradition sets out that the language died quickly, within two generations, and that the death was precipitated by the introduction of an English-language Bible in the church on Foula in 1740. The tradition is likely to be correct. We know that language death occurs quickly – sometimes in just a single generation – and the example of Cornish shows that the failure to provide Bible and Prayer Book in a language (in effect failing to make it a written language) did cause its demise. The situation where the introduction of English within the church has led to language decline is therefore well recorded. This is a major cause, for example, of the decline of Scots Gaelic, a language which was for long without a Bible, and in the death of Cornish, a language into which the Bible was never translated.

Today almost everyone sees language death as undesirable. For linguists the loss of a language represents the loss of a unique form of expression particularly suited to a specific culture, and therefore the loss of an irreplaceable insight into the functioning of human language, consciousness and society. For the maintenance of a culture, language and identity are intimately linked. In the British Isles we have in the last century or so seen the enormous efforts to preserve the Irish and Welsh languages as state-supported languages which are perceived as cornerstones of Irish and Welsh culture and identity. Scots Gaelic has received far less support than these, though still a considerable level of assistance as measured against its few speakers. The link between the Gaelic language and the culture of the West Highlands and Hebrides is strong, and many are seeking to strengthen it. Were Orkney and Shetland Norn alive today, there is no doubt that we would be making most strenuous efforts to preserve it.

Yet the people who have least care about the preservation of a dying language are often the speakers themselves. Frequently dying languages are seen as linked with poverty and lack of opportunity, and their loss is seen as an inevitable part of progress, and something which is to be encouraged. Children have often been discouraged from speaking the language, while schools and the church use only the replacement language. Orkney and Shetland Norn received just this sort of response from its last speakers. On Foula at least one informant called it 'that old dirt', while again on Foula the language was referred to with contempt as 'Da Dansk'. This last name is illuminating. Orkney and Shetland Norn must have been called something by its speakers, though their name for the language is not now recorded. They certainly didn't call it Dansk or Danish. By no stretch of the imagination is Orkney and Shetland Norn Danish. Such a wilfully perverse name is an expression of contempt for the language.

By around 1800, perhaps even earlier, it is usually argued that Orkney and Shetland Norn had ceased to be a language of everyday communication even on Foula. George Low, visiting Foula in 1774, is aware that he is recording something which is fast dying. Yet fragments of Norn have survived until much later, which is an argument for the continuance of mother-tongue speakers into the nineteenth century. It was even possible for a verse in the language to be collected as late 1958, and in 2007 the 'Foula Heritage' community website is still able to present the world with previously unknown fragments of the language. A very distant echo of the language may still be heard on Foula.

4

Texts in Orkney and Shetland Norn

ORKNEY AND SHETLAND Norn must be regarded not as a form of Old Norse which happened to be spoken in Orkney and Shetland, but as an independent language with its own identity. As with all languages, it is a unique reflection of the culture and community that created it. It is sad that so little has survived of language, culture and community, yet at least we have something. Those few texts which we possess are especially precious not as further examples of Old Norse or Norn, but as the sole record of the independent language Orkney and Shetland Norn.

In dealing with the remains of the language, problems abound. So little survives written in Orkney and Shetland Norn that we are without a convention for spelling. Because some recorders have equated it with Old Norse, they have sought to use the spelling conventions for Old Norse – or for one of its descendant languages, Faroese, Icelandic or Norwegian. This is a distortion. Other recorders have been unfamiliar with Old Norse, and have recorded what they thought they heard. Inevitably this has created curious spellings. The problem of the low quality of transcriptions is particularly acute because we have no 'good' text to use as a standard to tidy up the transcriptions; instead we know all the transcriptions to be poor, and therefore in need of interpretation in order to read them.

An example of the problem is illustrated by the treatment of George Low's transcription of *The Ballad of Hildina* by the Norwegian linguist Marius Hægstad (1900). One stanza serves to illustrate. In Low's transcription of the Orkney and Shetland Norn it reads:

> In kimerin Iarlin
> U klapasse Hildina kidn;
> On de kidn quirto vara
> Vult doch, fiegan vara moch or fly din.

Hægstad claims to offer a revised transliteration, that is a revised spelling of the words, but instead of transliterating in fact translates this text into Old Norse, producing the stanza:

> In Kimer in Iarlin
> u klapa se Hildina onde kidn;
> 'Quirto vult doch fiegan
> moch or fy din?'

The first two lines do seem to have a close Old Norse equivalent, giving some support to Hægstad's contention that the language is Old Norse. However, the second two lines, as most of the ballad, are significantly different when translated into Old Norse. The exercise of translating into Old Norse in fact demonstrates clearly that the text is not in Old Norse – yet Hægstad uses the version he feels he can deduce from the text to argue exactly the opposite, asserting that Orkney and Shetland Norn is effectively Old Norse. His evidence could be better interpreted as a demonstration that

Orkney and Shetland Norn is a different language. Indeed, the lines could be translated into Anglo-Saxon, or Old High German, or Gothic and bear the same sort of superficial resemblance that Hægstad finds.

Much of the scholarly discussion about Orkney and Shetland Norn has been based not on the original transcriptions, but on transcriptions 'corrected' into Old Norse. Thus the myth that Orkney and Shetland Norn is just Old Norse has had full rein.

Jakob Jakobsen has on occasions preserved only his transcribed or translated version. Thus a rhyme he heard on Foula he has recorded 'corrected' by him into what is effectively Old Norse as:

> I have malt maeldra
> Ek hef malit min meldra minn
> I have supet usen ek hef sopat husin;
> Ende seve de sede lin
> Enn a sefr at saeta lin,
> And dene komene lusa
> ok dagrinn er kominn i ljos.

The translation into English usually given for these lines is itself imperfect (in length as much as anything else) but it is anyway a translation of an Old Norse translation of an original in Orkney and Shetland Norn:

> I have ground my morning-meal
> I have swept the floors
> till the old wife sleeps
> and the daylight is in the chimney.

If we are to understand the texts we have to stop filtering them through Old Norse.

4.1 THE LORD'S PRAYER

The Lord's Prayer has been recorded both in Orkney and in Shetland Norn. Superficially there are many differences between the two texts. However, many of these differences are no more than variants in the spelling used by the recorder. Just a few may reflect genuine differences in pronunciation between Orkney and Shetland forms. Given the separation between the communities on the two island groups, it is likely that some differences in accent did develop. Indeed, it would be reasonable to expect accent differences even between islands in the two groups, a state of affairs which developed in the Faroe Islands to the extent that by the nineteenth century half a dozen or more distinct accents of Faroese existed.

Both versions of the Lord's Prayer, but especially that from Shetland, show a significant admixture of English words. The liturgical nature of the Lord's Prayer is a feature which would usually be expected to preserve old forms. Today millions of English speakers pray using a form of the Lord's Prayer which embodies early seventeenth-century grammar and diction: 'Our Father which art in heaven, hallowed be Thy name . . .', and many are resistant to efforts to update the prayer to reflect the language conventions of twenty-first-century English. That these two versions of the Lord's Prayer are in a progressive, English-influenced dialect suggests that they are late forms of Orkney and Shetland Norn.

THE LORD'S PRAYER IN ORKNEY NORN

Favor i ir i chimrie,
Helleur ir i nam thite,
gilla cosdum thite cumma,
veya thine mota vara gort
o yurn sinna gort i chimrie,
ga vus da on da dalight brow vora
Firgive vus sinna vora
sin vee Firgive sindara mutha vus,

> lyv vus ye i tumtation,
> min delivera vus fro olt ilt,
> Amen.

THE LORD'S PRAYER IN SHETLAND NORN

This is the form recorded by George Low on Foula. He describes his informant simply as 'an old woman'.

> Fy vor o er i Chimeri.
> Halaght vara nam dit.
> La Konungdum din cumma.
> La vill din vera guerde
> i vrildin senda eri chimeri.
> Gav vus dagh u dagloght brau.
> Forgive sindor wara sin
> vi forgiva gem ao sinda gainst wus.
> Lia wus eke o vera tempa,
> but delivra wus fro adlu idlu
> for doi ir Konungdum, u puri, u glori,
> Amen.

4.2 SIR ORFEO

Probably the best-known Orkney and Shetland Norn text is the two lines preserved as lines 2 and 4 within the refrain of a Scots rendering of the story of Sir Orfeo:

> Der lived a king inta da aste,
> Scowan ürla grün;
> Der lived a lady in da wast,
> Whar giorten han grün oarlac.

The traditional translation of the two lines is 'The wood is early green' and 'Where the hart goes yearly'. Quite what this has to do with either the king in the east or the lady in the west is open to conjecture, but as tradition supports the translation there is no particular reason to doubt it.

4.3 THE CUNNINGSBURGH PHRASE

The verse was recorded by George Low and collected by him from an informant in Cunningsburgh on Mainland Shetland.

> Myrk in e liora
> Luce in e liunga
> Timin e guest in
> Eeeee geungna!

> It is dark in the chimney
> There is light on the heather
> It is time the guest inside
> OUT should go!

Guests at Cunningsburgh should not overstay their welcome! When the fire is out and the sun has risen and lights the heather it is time for guests to be on their way. The verse only scans if the 'Eeeee' of the final line is prolonged for two beats, a device that neatly emphasises the word 'out'. The details of the translation are problematic. Is 'myrk' a noun ('dark') or an adjective ('darkness')? Similarly, does 'luce' mean 'light' or 'lightness'? The form 'in e' in lines 1 and 2 could mean 'is in the' or even 'still in the' (with the verb implied). The form 'e' may even be an English-influenced reduced form of the definite article 'the'. Yet, with all these translation problems, the verse still makes sense as a humorous injunction to guests not to overstay their welcome.

4.4 GEORGE LOW'S VOCABULARY

George Low presents a list of terms referring to the everyday life of people on Foula, which he collected from informants there. It is clear that few of these words are Lowland Scots forms. Equally clear, though seemingly not previously noted, is that many of the words bear little relationship to Old Norse. Rather they are forms unique to Orkney and Shetland Norn.

Foula	Fugla or Uttrie
island	hion
bread	coust
oat bread	corka coust
barley bread	boga coust
sea	sheug
fish	fisk
haddock	hoissan
cod	gronge grodningar
ling	longo
herring	sildin
rock	berg berrie
boat	bodin knorin
sail	seiglè
mast	mostin
coat	quot
shoe	seugin
stocking	sokin
cap	uga
sea maw or mew	whit fuglin
eagle	ednin
trencher or plate	bergesken
spoon	sponin
ladle	heosa
horse	hessin
mare	rupa
cow	kurin
sheep	fie sedvite
ewe	oron
pot	posney

4.5 THE BALLAD OF HILDINA

The outstanding text in Orkney and Shetland Norn is *The Ballad of Hildina*.

Our source is again George Low. As elsewhere, all of his spellings are idiosyncratic, and are influenced both by English, and by the conventions for spelling French, a language that Low knew something of. He is frequently unsure where word divisions should come.

The name of the original author of *The Ballad of Hildina* is unknown. As a folk ballad it is possible that the verses developed over years with the contributions of many in the community. This is not written literature but rather an oral composition within a largely illiterate community. George Low's version is believed to be the first and only time the song was written down, and his account specifically indicates that his informant was illiterate and therefore unable to help him with spelling.

The date of original composition is as problematic as its authorship. One answer is that there is no simple date for any oral composition which lives with a community, as pieces are added and changed through the years. That said, the language is remarkable for its preservation of early forms – indeed, there is very little in the poem that can be regarded as Scots or English. This seems to argue for an early date, and therefore for a long period of oral preservation.

The story told is specific to Orkney, recounting events in the life of an Earl of Orkney, though remembered and collected in Shetland. Presumably the ballad was once common throughout both Orkney and Shetland, and is an example of the cultural and linguistic unity which existed between the two island groups. Quite which earl is referred to is not clear from the poem. First impressions may suggest one of the dynasty of Norse jarls, though there is nothing to exclude the later Scottish earls, as these maintained connections with the Norwegian court. The named characters, Hildina and Hiluge, cannot be identified. *Hild* is a feminine suffix on many Germanic names, and might well be just part of a name. Alternatively it means little more than 'the maiden'.

There is a reference in the ballad to St Magnus' Church in Kirkwall. This may of course be a later addition to the poem, but if taken at face value must indicate a date subsequent to the building of St

Magnus' Cathedral. Earl Magnus died in 1117, executed on the orders of his cousin Earl Hakon, dying what came to be regarded as a martyr's death. The miracles associated with his relics led to his prompt beatification and the building of his cathedral in the mid-twelfth century through the efforts of his brother-in-law Kol and nephew Rognvald. If the earl of the ballad is one of the Norwegian dynasty, the events of the poem cannot be earlier than the late twelfth century – nor much later either, for the Norwegian dynasty soon failed. If he is an earl of the Scottish dynasty, the poem could describe events from the thirteenth or fourteenth centuries. It is hard to see how the cultural milieu of the poem could be much later than the fourteenth century. I suggest, therefore, oral transmission for at least 400 years, and perhaps as many as 600 years. The evidence of oral transmission elsewhere in the world is that very long periods are possible, and I see no reason to question this time frame. That said, an oral transmission of twelve to eighteen generations is a remarkable cultural achievement.

The ballad as preserved is clearly faulty, in that some of the lines are too long or too short, while in very many places the rhyme fails. Indeed, in working with the poem it is easy to feel that there are more scansion faults than correct instances. Possibly the folk style did not place as much importance on consistency of rhyme as we tend to. The difficulties of translation are substantial, and in parts its meaning is opaque.

There are also difficulties in detail. For example, Hildina is taken from a 'glass pavilion' in Norway, something which seems most unlikely ever to have existed. Perhaps there is a solution in the concept of the medieval solar, the women's room of a prestigious residence which may have had glazed windows.

For the preservation of the poem we are indebted to George Low. This poem, along with other Orkney and Shetland Norn fragments and observations on the language, is found in his manuscript published more than a century later as *A Tour Through the Islands of Orkney and Schetland: Containing Hints Relative to their Ancient, Modern*

and Natural History, Collected in 1774. The publishers were William
Peace and Son of Kirkwall, 1879. George Low's description of the
Ballad of Hildina deserves to be set out in full:

> The following song is the most entire I could find, but the disorder
> of some of the stanzas will show that it is not wholly so. The subject
> is a strife between a King of Norway and an Earl of Orkney, on ac-
> count of the hasty marriage of the Earl with the King's daughter in
> her father's absence. Here it is worthy to be observed that most of
> the fragments they have are old historical Ballads and Romances,
> this kind of poetry being more greedily swallowed and retentively
> preserved by memory than any others, and most fitted to the genius
> of the Northerns. In this Ballad I cannot answer for the orthogra-
> phy. I wrote it as an old man pronounced it; nor could he assist me
> in this particular. This man (William Henry, a farmer in Guttorm,
> in Foula) has the most knowledge of any I found; he spoke of three
> kinds of poetry used in Norn, and repeated or sung by the old men;
> the Ballad (or Romance, I suppose); the Vysie or Vyse, now com-
> monly sung to dancers; and the simple Song. By the account he
> gave of the matter, the first seems to have been valued here chiefly
> for its subject, and was commonly repeated in winter by the fireside;
> the second seems to have been used in publick meetings, now only
> sung to the dance; and the third at both. Let it be remarked that the
> following ballad may be either written in two long line or four short
> line stanzas.

George Low's account presents the ballad, then notes:

A literal translation of the above I could not procure,
but the substance is this:
   'An Earl of Orkney, in some of his rambles on the coast of Norway,
saw and fell in love with the King's daughter of the country. As their
passion happened to be reciprocal, he carried her off in her father's
absence, who was engaged in war with some of his distant neighbours.
On his return, he followed the fugitives to Orkney, accompanied by
his army, to revenge on the Earl the rape of his daughter. On his arrival there, Hildina (which was her name), first spied him, and advised
her now husband to go and attempt to pacify the King. He did so,

and by his appearance and promise brought the King so over as to be satisfied with the match. This, however, was of no long standing, for as soon as the Earl's back was turned a courtier, called Hiluge, took great pains to change the King's mind, for it seems Hiluge had formerly hoped to succeed with the daughter himself. His project took, and the matter came to blows; the Earl is killed by Hiluge, who cut off his head and threw it at his lady, which, she says, vexed her even more than his death, that he should add cruelty to revenge. Upon the Earl's death, Hildina is forced to follow her father to Norway, and in a little time Hiluge makes his demand to have her in marriage of her father; he consents, and takes every method to persuade Hildina, who, with great reluctance, agrees upon condition that she is allowed to fill the wine at her wedding. This is easily permitted, and Hildina infuses a drug which soon throws the company into a dead sleep, and after ordering her father to be removed, set the house on fire. The flame soon rouses Hiluge, who piteously cries for mercy, but the taunts he had bestowed at the death of the Earl of Orkney are now bitterly returned, and he is left to perish in the flames.'

Such is the subject of the Ballad, which might have been built on a true story, tho' now lost. It, however, shews the genius of the people, that tho' they were cut off from the rest of the world they had amusements, and these correspondent to the manners of the Northerns, among whom nothing was more common than the recital of the acts of their fathers. Most of all their tales are relative to the history of Norway; they seem to know little of the rest of Europe but by names; Norwegian transactions they have at their fingers' ends.

The text of *The Ballad of Hildina* as recorded by George Low – and therefore in Orkney and Shetland Norn – is given here:

Da vara Jarlin d'Orkneyar
For frinda sĭn spur de ro
Whirdi an skildè meun
Our glas buryon burtaga.

Or vanna ro eidnar fuo
Tega du meun our glas buryon
Kere friendè min yamna men
Eso vrildan stiendi gede min vara to din.

Yom keimir cullingin
Fro liene burt
Asta Vaar hon fruen Hildina
Hemi stu mer stien.

Whar an yaar elonden
Ita kan sadnast wo
An scal vara kundè
Wo osta tre sin reithin ridna dar fro

Kemi to Orkneyar Jarlin
Vilda mien sante Maunis
I Orknian u bian sian
I lian far diar.

An gevè Drotnign kedn puster
On de kin firsane furu
Tworare wo eder
Whitranè kidn.

In kimerin Jarlin
U klapasse Hildina
On de kidn quirto
Vult doch, fiegan vara moch or fly din.

Elde vilda fiegan vara
Fy min u alt sin
Ans namnu wo
So minyach u ere min heve Orkneyar kingè ro.

Nu di skall taga dor yochwo
And u ria dor to strandane nir
U yilsa fy minu avon
Blit an ear ne cumi i dora band.

Nu Swaran Konign
So mege gak honon i muthi
Whath ear di ho gane mier
I daute buthe.

Tretti merkè vath ru godle
Da skall yach ger yo

U all de vara sonna less
So linge sin yach liva mo.

Nu linge stug an konign
U linge wo a swo
Wordig vaar dogh mugè sonè
Yacha skier fare moga so minde yach angan u frien
Rost wath comman mier to landa.

Nu swara Hiluge
Hera geve honon scam
Taga di gild firre Hildina
Sin yach skall liga dor fram.

Estin whaar u feur fetign
Agonga kadn i sluge
Feur fetign sin gonga
Kadn i pluge.

Nu stienderin Jarlin.
U linge wo an wo
Dese mo eke Orknear
So linge san yach lava mo.

Nu eke tegaran san
Sot Koningn fyrin din
U alt yach an Hilhugin
Widn ugare din arar.

Nu swarar an frauna Hildina
U dem san idne i fro
Di slo dor a bardagana
Dar comme ov sin mo.

Nu Jarlin an genger
I vadlin fram
U kadnar sina mien
Geven skeger i Orkneyan.

Han u cummin
In u vod lerdin

Fronde fans lever
Vel burne mun.

Nu fruna Hildina
On genger i vadlin fram
Fy di yera da ov man dum
Dora di spidlaikì mire man.

Nu sware an Hiluge
Crego gevan a scam
Gayer an Jarlin frinde
Din an u fadlin in.

Nu fac an Jarlin dahuge
Dar min de an engine gro
An east ans huge ei
Fong ednar u vaxhedne more neo.

Di lava mir gugna
Yift bal yagh fur o lande
Gipt mir nu fruan Hildina
Vath godle u fasta bande.

Nu bill on heve da yals
Guadnè borè u da kadn
Sina kloyn a bera do skall
Fon fruna Hildina verka wo sino chelsina villya.

Hildina liger wo chaldona
U o dukrar u grothè
Min du buga till bridlevsin
Bonlother u duka dogha.

Nu Hildina on askar feyrin
Sien di gava mier livè
Ou skinka vin
Ou guida vin.

Duska skinka vin, u guida vin
Tinka dogh eke wo
Jarlin an gougha here din.

Watha skilde tinka
Wo Jarlin gouga herè min
Hien minde yagh inga forlskona
Bera fare kera fyrin min.

Da gerde on fruna Hildina
On bar se mien ot
On soverin fest,
Fysin u quarsin sat.

Da gerde un fruna Hildina
On bard im ur
Hadlin burt sien on laghdè
Gloug I osta jatha port.

Nu iki visti an Hiluge
Ike ov till do
Eldin var commin i lut
U stor u silkè sark ans smo.

Nu leveren fram
Hiluge du kereda
Fraun Hildina du
Gevemir live u gre

So mege u gouga gre
Skall dogh swo
Skall lathì min heran
I bardagana fwo.

Du tuchtada lide undocht yach
Swo et sa ans bugin bleo
Dogh casta ans huge
I mit fung u vexemir mise meo.

Nu tachtè on heve fwelsko
Ans bo vad mild u stien
Dogh skall aidè misè Koningnsens
Vadna vilda mien.

The poem is a translator's nightmare! One approach has been to rewrite the poem as if it were Old Norse, then to translate this. The 'corrected' Old Norse text is given by Dr M. Hægstad in his edition of *The Ballad of Hildina* contained in *Skrifter udgivne af Videnskabs-selskabet i Christiania*, 1900 (*Historisk-Filosofiske Klasse*, II). This can then be translated. An English translation of the first twelve verses (only) does exist and reads as follows:

It was the Earl from Orkney,
And counsel of his kin sought he,
Whether he should the maiden
Free from her misery.

'If thou free the maid from her gleaming hall,
O kinsman dear of mine,
Ever while the world shall last
Thy glory still shall shine.'

Home came the king,
Home from the ship's levy
The lady Hildina she was gone,
And only her stepmother there found he.

'Be he in whatever land,
This will I prove true,
He shall be hanged from the highest tree
That ever upward grew.'

'If the Earl but come to Orkney,
Saint Magnus will be his aid,
And in Orkney ever he will remain –
Haste after him with speed.'

The King he stood before his lady,
And a box on her ear gave he, –
And all adown her lily white cheeks
The tears did flow truly.

The Earl he stood before Hildina,
And a pat on her cheek gave he, –

'O which of us two wouldst thou have lie dead,
Thy father dear or me?'

'I would rather see my father doomed,
And all his company,
If so my own true lord and I
May long rule in Orkney.

'Now do thou take in hand thy steed,
And ride thou down to the strand;
And do thou greet my sire full blithely,
And gladly will he clasp thy hand.'

The King he now made answer –
So sore displeased was he –
'In payment for my daughter
What will thou give to me?'

'Thirty marks of the red gold,
This to thee will I give,
And never shalt thou lack a son
As long as I may live.'

Now long stood the King,
And long on the Earl gazed he:–
'O thou art worth a host of sons;
Thy boon is granted thee.'

An alternative method for translation is to look at Germanic roots. My own effort below is based on this philological methodology, and produces the following version (of the whole ballad):

Once upon a time the Earl of Orkney asked his brother
'From out her glass pavilion should I steal our King's daughter?'
'My brother if you take this maiden from out her glass pavilion
Your deed shall be remembered for years a million million.'
Thus when the King came home from Viking voyage a winner
The stepmother was still at home, but there was no Hildina.
'I swear by all that's holy that wherever he may be
I'll hang him by his neck from the very highest tree.'

To good St Magnus' Church in Orkney fled the Earl,
To Orkney sped the King, to save his little girl.
Meeting the married lady there he boxed her round the ears
Soon down her white cheeks there flowed a flood of tears.
The Earl embraced Hildina, and kissed her on the cheek,
'My darling wife, between us two, whose death would you now
   seek?'
'Not to my father but to you I swore my lasting vow,
And so by that we both may rule, us two in Orkney now.

'Go to your horse and overtake my father on the beach,
Greet him kindly, clasp hands, his blessing to beseech.'
The King made a stern reply, his anger did not falter,
'I want to know what bride price can you give me for my daughter?'
'Thirty marks of burnished gold shall I unto you give,
And you will never lack a son for as long as I may live.'
Long stood the King, gazed on the Earl for long,
'You're worth a thousand sons my man, though what you did was
   wrong.'

Now among the King's companions was the swarthy Hiluge,
To wed the beauteous Hildina his dream for many a day.
Again and again and craftily Hiluge spoke to the King,
Again and again the King did listen, once more to this thing.
Now for a long time the King looked at the Earl standing near
'You may not, Orkney; a long time ago I betrothed my daughter dear.'
'I will take nothing against his will from the King your father,
Instead to give Hiluge his rights, that would I rather.'

Hildina looked from the one to the other, turned pale,
One would die in the fight, that fate would not fail.
Now the Earl stepped forward onto the duelling ground
And the King turned his face from Orkney, looked around.
'Now one of us must die, 'tis either thee or me',
The blows rained down, down fell the Earl Orkney.
Now Lady Hildina steps on the grass where soon a corpse must lie,
'Father by all that's holy do not let a brave man die.'

But Hiluge answered her: 'Call Odin's maidens here,
For death draws nigh the Earl, this man your husband dear.

Now the Earl felt the axe bite through his neck, a clean kill
Hiluge threw the head into her arms; she grew more angry still.
'You promised me marriage if I voyaged far from our land
Now with golden dowry and strong vows give me Hildina's hand.'
Now were her eyes downcast as she looked upon the King
For the lady Hildina against her will must take a golden ring.

Soon that time came, though Hildina wished it never,
With that man to be joined, husband and wife forever.
Now Hildina asked her father 'May I serve the wine,
Choose who will get the best, who the worst, when we come to dine?'
'Both the best and the worst as you rightly think,
Both earls and freemen this day must drink.'
A drugged wine she gave them, both to earls and to freemen,
Their eyes were heavy, sleep came over them.

Then the Lady Hildina went in, her face was set,
She saw her father and the guests asleep, on the benches where they
     sat.
Then the Lady Hildina went in, dragged her father across the floor,
Laid him on the grass outside and fastened close the door.
Now Hiluge awakes as the fire begins to rage,
The smoke is black and thick, the banquet hall a cage.
Now a scream breaks from the throat of Hiluge,
'Oh Lady Hildina, let me live another day.'

'So may you cry out, now you should believe,
That same mercy you showed in the battle you shall receive,
You did not care for him or me, that was clear for all to see,
That you threw his head at me, that angered me.
Now receive a heavy fate, for soon to death you yield,
The king cannot help you now, on this battlefield.'
All this for once upon a time the Earl of Orkney asked his brother
'From out her glass pavilion should I steal our King's daughter?'

The Ballad of Hildina has been noted by commentators as a curious text, and treated purely in this light. No one appears to have
examined its literary merits, which are of some significance. This is
a poem with many qualities.

There are of course caveats associated with attempting any sort of literary criticism of this poem. The text we have is fragmentary. There are verses that are too long and some that are too short, and sections where the rhythm fails. In working with the song I have felt that there are most probably lost lines or even whole verses lost, as the action sometimes advances suddenly with the reader struggling to fill the gaps of what has happened. Everything that survives has been filtered through George Low's transcription, and the inevitable errors he introduced. Additionally, the translation problems are severe. George Low had been provided with a very brief synopsis of the story, not a line-by-line translation, and the efforts of scholars working on the poem in subsequent years have not negated this deficiency. My own translation attempts a readable narrative, though in doing so interprets freely and should probably be regarded as a retelling of the story. While I cannot better the accuracy of previous translations, I can easily criticise them – as others will be able to criticise my efforts. They, like my translation, are full of errors. The philological method utilised to get a meaning from this text lacks precision, and while I have no doubt that a large team of many-skilled experts could advance our knowledge, it seems unlikely that *The Ballad of Hildina* will receive this sort of attention. What we have therefore is a fragmentary and corrupted text in a largely unrecorded, dead language and which can only be interpreted through the arcane discipline of philology.

The established convention of transcription of this poem, following George Low, has been to present it as thirty-five four-line stanzas. Thus the poem is made to conform to an English verse form with which we are familiar. A brief examination shows that this stanza format is inappropriate: *The Ballad of Hildina* simply doesn't fit. While there is some sort of rhyming scheme operating, even taking into account the deficiencies of our text, that scheme cannot be regarded as consistent. Typically only two lines within a four-line verse rhyme; most often these are the second and fourth line, though there are very many exceptions. Similarly there is great irregularity in the length of individual lines, and as a consequence there are breaks in the rhythm of the poem. It seems to me that there is a case for recasting *The Ballad of Hildina* in long lines which rhyme in couplets. This improves the rhyming consistency somewhat, and has a positive effect on the rhythm. The form is still not perfect, but does at least seem to be an improvement. The rhythmic pause in the middle of the resulting long lines – the caesura – is familiar in early Germanic verse, particularly Anglo-Saxon, though largely absent from later English writing. This style of long lines in pairs is the format I have adopted for my own translation.

From the perspective of literary criticism it is worth noting that *The Ballad of Hildina* does not follow an established poetic format that is either English or Norse. Rather there is a case for seeing it as a style which developed within Orkney and Shetland Norn. We have in *The Ballad of Hildina* a hint of a distinctive Orkney and Shetland Norn poetic style.

The ballad is remarkably free from imagery. Poetry of early Germanic languages abounds in simile and metaphor. Anglo-Saxon developed the poetic style of kennings, where images of two or three words are used to refer to often simple concepts, and as set phrases could easily be assembled within a poem. The ability to produce such images was what was expected from a poet. In Old Icelandic verse image is piled on image to create a verse of great complexity, often more riddle and language game than sentence. Yet here in *The Ballad of Hildina* we have a poem which is all but free of images. It is in a different tradition to the verse forms of Iceland and Norway, and while the theme is Norse the tradition is specific to Orkney and Shetland Norn.

The description of the poem as a ballad is apt. It falls within the tradition of a sung love story, a form which blossomed in the Middle Ages throughout Europe, and has continued – though with less vigour – to today. Save for its conformity to this basic style, it is difficult to put labels on the poem. It is certainly not Christian in inspiration or values. The only Christian reference appears accidental, for while the Earl of Orkney and Hildina marry in Kirkwall in St Magnus' Church, for the sake of the narrative they could as easily have married in a Viking ceremony. The ballad is not within the Icelandic saga tradition, as the historical dimension is missing. Neither Earl of Orkney nor King of Norway is identified, while if Hildina is a real person there are no clues by which to identify her. It is not a debate on moral values; it is not a lyric which prioritises form over content. It is something else. And in that quality of being something else the poem finds its place as a distinctive literary contribution.

Nevertheless, there is a need to try to classify it as a way of understanding it. It seems to me that what we have here is not something within the English or Continental tradition which goes back ultimately to classical models, but rather a Germanic heroic poem. It owes more to the spirit of the Anglo-Saxon *Beowulf* than to anything that comes later, yet in its way its heroic milieu transcends even that of *Beowulf*; it is more completely Germanic than even *Beowulf*.

It has for long been regretted that we have no true examples of the earliest Germanic oral literature. Everything we have has been filtered through the literary traditions of the churchmen who wrote them down. The Icelandic sagas all post-date the advent of Christianity, and even the overt retelling of Norse myths is set beside the Christian story, so that we are viewing the action through a Christian perspective. From Old High German little has survived that is original literature as opposed to translation. From Anglo-Saxon the presumed corpus of authentic pre-Christian Germanic literature has been reduced by recent scholarly study to almost nothing, perhaps literally nothing. The majority of Anglo-Saxon literature is overtly Christian, while that which does not claim to be Christian didacticism is probably Christian allegory. Thus *Beowulf*, once regarded as the grand epic of pagan Germanic culture, may now be regarded as a Christian allegory (and what is worse one where the allegory is poorly made), while the *Elegies* are now usually seen as conveying Christian moral values. Against this background *The Ballad of Hildina* stands as the only Germanic poem to be preserved through an unsullied oral tradition and written down without the intervention of the church. Orkney and Shetland Norn provides the sole example of an unfiltered pagan, heroic, Germanic literature.

The ethical values of *The Ballad of Hildina* are that of the heroic code. The Earl of Orkney knows that eloping with Hildina will have terrible consequences, but does it anyway so that his name will be remembered. This action is nowhere criticised. Rather there is a Germanic craving for one's name to be remembered by the poets, and even implicit approval for his action. When the King of Norway arrives in Orkney, the Earl knows that the likely consequence is the death of one or the other. The Earl asks Hildina to choose. Had she chosen her father, the heroic code in which he is living would have forced him to surrender to the King and accept execution. There is a good, heroic Orkney precedent for such behaviour in the meek manner in which Earl Magnus – St Magnus – met his death at the hands of his cousin. When the King ultimately decides in favour of Hiluge, the Earl accepts his fate without demur. He does not plead his case or beg for his life. His beheading is at the hands of his rival, quick and brutal. The ballad presents a contrast between on the one hand the forgiving acceptance by the King of a marriage he did not want for his daughter, and on the other the heroic bonds of society which mean Hiluge's interests cannot be set aside. In the ballad there is no contest – heroic values win over forgiveness. While Hiluge to our way of thinking is the villain of the poem, he is also a man playing a natural part within the society in which he lived, and his right to behead the Earl is acknowledged by everyone. Had he not acted as he did he would have been dishonoured. Hildina's anger at him is less at the beheading than at his action in throwing the severed head at her. The heroic value system does not require this gesture; rather it is simple brutality and it is this that is the motive for Hildina's revenge.

The outstanding character of the ballad is Hildina. Anglo-Saxon literature is completely without strong female characters in the heroic poems, and even in the saints' lives, where women play their part, their roles are frequently that of enduring suffering. Old Icelandic literature does have some positive female roles, though these are infrequent. Both Anglo-Saxon and Old Icelandic female stereotypes reflect the European early medieval literary convention that was a product of the early church. It is remarkable that our one substantial survival in Orkney and Shetland Norn from an oral tradition features a woman in such a prominent role. Within the short length of the poem her character emerges as both complex and strong.

In the elopement Hildina's role appears passive, though it is nowhere suggested that she does not consent to it. George Low's informant seemed to have additional information about the story not contained in the version recorded, which is that the Earl and Hildina were already acquainted. Her marriage vows appear freely made, and she affirms them afterwards, declaring her allegiance to her husband rather than to her father – a situation paralleled by Desdemona in Shakespeare's *Othello*. As the action develops she becomes ever more proactive. It is Hildina who urges reconciliation between the Earl and her father, Hildina who pleads with her father for his life, Hildina who is angered by Hiluge's brutality. As the action shifts to Norway it is Hildina who makes a plan for the brutal murder of Hiluge and many others, Hildina who plays the active role of poisoning the wine, and Hildina who drags her sleeping father from the room. Nowhere is she criticised for her actions; rather the heroic code appears to accept it as appropriate. Hiluge's plea for his life is an opportunity for her to explain that her action is revenge in the form of Hiluge's life for the life of the Earl, and implicitly this is accepted. That the wedding guests are also to die is ignored, almost as if it is unimportant.

I cannot bring to mind a medieval or renaissance text in which a woman is so clearly the protagonist, or in which such barbaric slaughter is accepted and even implicitly applauded. These are values of the

Germanic world. Here we see the heroic revenge ethic, within a code which sees remembrance of a heroic life as an end in itself. In that the poem has survived, the Earl and Hildina both have their immortality.

What truth there may be in the story told is of course speculation. Shockingly, the story may well be true. House burnings abound in the history of the Viking world as a part of feuds which could last for centuries. The best known is the house burning in the Icelandic *Burnt-Njal's Saga*, a tragedy which probably did happen much as set out in the saga. Indeed, such events were sufficiently commonplace that it is quite possible that a medieval wedding feast in Norway was ended by the events described in *The Ballad of Hildina*, and for it to be unremembered in the historical record today.

4.6 Jakobsen's Foula Fragments

Jakobsen recorded the following verse on Foula in 1897, which he 'corrected' to conform with Old Norse. He pointed out that it is a variant of a verse known on the Faroe Islands, and called there 'Gryla'. As Jakobsen records it ('corrected' to Old Norse models) it is:

> Skekla komena rina tuna
> swarta hæsta blæta bruna
> fo'mtena (fjo'mtan) hala
> and fo'mtena (fjo'mtan) bjadnis a kwara hala.

> Skekla rides to the homestead on a black horse with a white blaze and fifteen tails, and fifteen children on each tail.

The song recalls a familiar story from Norse mythology where the female ogre Skekla riding a many-tailed horse encourages children to grab onto a tail, then rides off with them.

4.7 The Last Text in Orkney and Shetland Norn

A verse was recorded on Foula in 1958 which is conventionally regarded as the last living memory of Orkney and Shetland Norn.

The informant was George Isbister (nicknamed Dodie). The verse reads:

> Ante pedu, sat a growla
> Sat a growla festa,
> Pirla moga, hench a boga,
> Settar alla nesta.

This appears to be a fragment of a song known in the Faroes and elsewhere and called 'The Eagle Song'. The sound of the lines is memorable, though their sense is elusive.

4.8 SURVIVING FRAGMENTS

Jakob Jakobsen believed he had collected the very last survival of Orkney and Shetland Norn, in the greeting 'halgat varit' which an elderly informant used. The extinction of Orkney and Shetland Norn should mark a terminus for the collection of materials in the language. Yet even today new fragments can emerge. A 2007 website for Foula – www.foulaheritage.org.uk – includes fragments of Orkney and Shetland Norn previously unrecorded.

Fragments indeed! The final gleaning is the lines:

> Teedna barna, teedna barna,
> Vilna vant . . .
> . . . neesta vagel.

This is part of a lullaby, and 'teedna barna' means 'quiet child' – the rest is perhaps too fragmentary to attempt translation. Possibly even today someone, somewhere has further fragments of a largely lost language.

5

Impact

Historians from the classical world and the early Middle Ages say that the Early English reached Orkney and Shetland. Their claims are confirmed by the traces of pre-Viking forms in the indigenous language Orkney and Shetland Norn. The Early English take their place as one of the many early peoples to have settled in the islands, and to have contributed to their distinctive culture.

There are implications for our understanding of the history and culture of the British Isles. The English migration included not just the south of the islands – the part we now call England – but a much larger area, including the furthest north. In this as in so many other areas of early settlement it becomes clear that the British Isles are a single coherent unit, and that from Kent to Shetland the settlement patterns have more similarities than differences.

There are implications too for the culture of Orkney and Shetland. The indigenous language Orkney and Shetland Norn is not just a variant of Old Norse, but rather a form of speech that developed on the islands and which represents the first Early English settlers as well as the later Viking settlers. Orkney and Shetland have a language unique to the islands.

Perhaps too we should re-examine the texts that remain in the language, particularly *The Ballad of Hildina*. Here we have a competent literary work which deserves a wider readership. Additionally we have the only piece of old Germanic literature which has reached us direct from an oral tradition rather than filtered through the rewriting of early churchmen. *The Ballad of Hildina* offers an important glimpse into a now lost literary style.

The concept of Early English settlement of Orkney and Shetland adds new wealth to the already rich culture of Orkney and Shetland.

Sources

This book uses a range of secondary sources, as well as primary research into aspects of the Norn Language of Orkney and Shetland.

The secondary sources have not been individually referenced. They are part of the accepted view of the early and medieval history of the islands, and can readily be found in published work, including such online sources as the encyclopaedia Wikipedia. What is new is their assemblage in order to demonstrate the place of the Early English settlement.

The primary research is within the area of Orkney and Shetland Norn. While the failure of *i*-mutation has been noted previously (by Michael P. Barnes, 1998) its ramifications have not been considered. Nor am I aware of any previous work which compares and contrasts Orkney and Shetland Norn with Anglo-Saxon, or indeed which considers Orkney and Shetland Norn as anything other than a dialect of Old Norse. The translations of Orkney and Shetland Norn are my own (save where otherwise stated) and represent a new contribution to appreciating the language. The literary discussion of *The Ballad of Hildina* is likewise my work, applying standard concepts of literary criticism and with minimal input from other writers.

The works listed in the bibliography below are those which lie behind this book. I have made no effort to produce an extensive bibliography of the subject; such are available through library catalogues in Kirkwall and Lerwick.

Bibliography

Balneaves, Elizabeth, *The Windswept Isles: Shetland and its People* (London, 1977)

Barnes, Michael P., 'Orkney and Shetland Norn', in Peter Trudgill, ed., *Language in the British Isles* (Cambridge, 1984)

Barnes, Michael P., *The Norn Language of Orkney and Shetland* (Lerwick, 1998)

Hibbert-Ware, Samuel, *A Description of the Shetland Islands* (Edinburgh, 1822)

Jakobsen, Jakob, *An Etymological Dictionary of the Norn Language in Shetland*, 2 vols (London and Copenhagen, 1928–32; repr. 1985)

Jakobsen, Jakob, *The Place-Names of Shetland* (London, 1936; translated by Anna Horsbøl from the original Danish: *Shetlandsøernes Stednavne*, first published 1901)

Kjorsvik Schei, Liv, and Moberg, Gunnie, *The Faroe Islands* (Edinburgh, 2003)

Lehmann, Eigil, 'Hildina-kvaedet. Ein etteroeknad og ei tolking by', *Fra Fjon til Fusa: Årbok for Hordamuseet og for Nord- og Midhordland sogelag* (1984)

Livingstone, W.P., *Shetland and the Shetlanders* (Edinburgh, 1947)

Low, George, *A Tour through the Islands of Orkney and Schetland: Containing Hints relative to their Ancient, Modern, and Natural History Collected in 1774* (Kirkwall, 1879)

Marwick, Hugh, *The Orkney Norn* (Oxford, 1929)

Mouat, Farley, *West Viking* (London, 1966)

Rendboe, Laurits, 'The Lord's Prayer in Orkney and Shetland Norn', *North-Western European Language Evolution* 14 (1989), 77–112 and 15 (1990), 49–111

Stewart, John, *Norn in Shetland* (Thorshaven, 1964)

Wallace, James, *An Account of the Islands of Orkney* (London, 1700)

Index

Adrianople, battle of, 21
Aesc, 46
Agricola, 11, 41
Aidan, saint, 15
America, 4, 63
Angles, 18, 40
Anglo-Saxon, 54, 119
Anglo-Saxon Chronicle, 45
Angus, 7, 27
Annals of Ulster, 30
antler, reindeer, 28
Antonine Wall, 12, 44
Athens, 64

Baghdad, 64
The Ballad of Hildina, 67, 102–20
Baltic Sea, 6
Basque, 7
Bede, 15
Beowulf, 117
Bergen, 4, 6
Bernicia, 27
Bible, 33

Bjarni Kolbeinsson, 47
Bradwell-on-Sea, 23
Brancaster, 23
Breton, 25
Bridei I, king, 15
Bridei MacBile, king, 30
Brechin, 27
bretwalder, 27
broch, 8-10
bronze age, 49
Bulgaria, 21
Burgh Castle, 23
Burnt Njal's Saga, 120

Caedmon, 16
caesura, 116
Caithness, 4, 32, 63, 65
Caledonii, 7
Candida Casa, 14
Cape Wrath, 4, 26
Carthage, 22
Celtic language, 7
Christian I, king, 33

Claudianus, Claudius, 38, 56
Claudius, emperor, 43
Columba, saint, 14, 15, 26–7
Copenhagen, 33
Cornish, 90, 92
Cornwall, 37
count of the Saxon Shore, 23
Crayford, 46
Crimean Gothic, 63
Cromarty Firth, 4, 26
crusades, 64
Cunningsburgh Phrase, 101

Dalmatia, 21
Danish, 61–2
Deira, 27
Denmark, 33
DNA, 1
Dover, 23
dratsie, 70
Dublin, 64
Dutch, 91

Ebbsfleet, 45
Ebusa, 43
Edinburgh, 27
Egypt, 36
Encyclopaedia Britannica, 58
England, 6
English, 91

Faroe Islands, 4, 6, 29, 63, 85, 89, 91, 99
Faroese, 60
Faroese philology, 68
Fife, 7
Firth of Forth, 15
Flateyjarbok, 31
Forth–Clyde valley, 3, 7, 39
Foula, 67, 93-4

Frankish kingdom, 22
Fraserburgh, 4

Gaelic, 24, 26, 90–1, 93–4
Galloway, 7
Gaukur Trandilsson, 64
Gaul, 22
Germania, 39
Germany, 6
Gibraltar, Straits of, 22
Goths, 21
grammar, 75
Great Caledonian Forest, 20
Great Glen, 14
Greece, 21
Greenland, 4, 29, 63
Guttorm, 105
Gypsy, 25, 54

Haakon VI Magnusson, king, 32
Hadrian's Wall, 12, 18, 20, 24
Haegstad, M, 97
Hakon, earl, 104
Hanseatic Ports, 6
Hantsholm, 6
Harald I Fair Hair, king, 30
Hebrides, 94
    Sea of, 4
Heimskringla, 17, 48
Hengist, 43, 44
Henry, William, 105
Herman, 52
Hermaness Hill, 52
heroic ethic, 120
heroic poetry, 117
Highlands, 7
    West, 94
Historia Brittonum, 42
Horsa, 42

i-mutation, 76–85
Iberia, 21
Ibister, George, 121
Iceland, 4, 51, 61, 63, 85
Icelandic, 61,
Inchcolm, 15, 26-7
Ingvaeonic, 18
Inverness, 15
Iona, 14, 15, 26
Ireland, 4, 13, 14, 32, 89
Irish, 7, 14, 90
Irish Annals of Tigernach, 30
iron age, 49
Isidore of Seville, saint, 41

Jakobsen, Jakob, 51, 67–70, 98, 101, 121
James I & VI, king, 33
James III, king, 33
Jarlshof, 49–50
Jerusalem, 48, 64
Jews, 22, 54
Joms-Vikings, 47–8
Jutes, 18
Juvenal, 41

kennings, 116
Kirkwall, 6, 103
Kol, 104

Latin, 25
Leith, 34
Lerwick, 4
Lindisfarne, 15
Linklater, Erik, 59
Loch Ness, 14
Lombards, 22
London, 20
longhouses, 49
Lord's Prayer, 72, 99

Lothian, 27
Low, George, 67, 95, 101–2, 115, 119
Lowland Scots, 33–4
Lympne, 23

Macedonia, 21
Maes Howe, 64
Magnus, earl and saint, 32, 104, 118
Man, Isle of, 42, 64
Manx, 90
Marcian, 45
Margaret of Norway, 33
Moesia, 21
Mons Graupius, 11-12
Mount Hekla, 65
Mousa, 9
Mousehole, 92

Nectaridus, 23
Nennius, 42, 47, 56, 58
neogrammarian tradition, 68
Netherlands, 6
Ninian, saint, 13, 24
Normandy, 64
Norn, 66
Norse gods, 32
North Sea, 20
Northumbria, 27
Norway, 31–2, 85
Norwegian, 62

Octa, 43
ogham, 7-8, 26
Olav Tryggvasson, 32
Old English, 83
Old High German, 83
Old Norse/Icelandic, 59, 60, 83, 90, 96

Oppenheimer, Stephen, 53
Origines, 41
Orkney, Earl of, 4, 30-1, 103
Orkney Museum, 28
Orkneyingasaga, 31
Ostrogoths, 21
Oswald, king of Northumbria, 15
Othello, 119

Pentreath, Dorothy, 92
Peterhead, 4
Pevensey, 23
Picts, 6–8, 12, 24–6, 29, 39, 43–4, 49, 56
place-names, 31–2
Pliny the Elder, 40
Portchester Castle, 23
Portuguese, 82
pronunciation, 78
Ptolemy, 36
Pytheas of Marseille, 37

Reculver, 23
Rheged, 13, 14
Rhine, river, 20, 22
Richborough, 23
Rognvald, 104
Roman Britain, 19
Romans, 11, 18–19, 40
Romany, 90
Rome, 13, 45, 64
    sack of, 21
Ross and Cromarty, 63
Rumelia, 21
Russia, 63
runic, 7, 17

Saami, 63
St Magnus' Cathedral, 32, 103, 117

St Ninian's Isle, 13
Saxa Vord, 52
Saxi, 52
Saxons, 18, 39, 40, 45
Saxon Shore, 19, 48
Scotland, 89
Scott, Sir Walter, 50
Seythisfjorthur, 6
Shelta, 90, 93
Shetland dialect, 69
ships, 28–9
    clinker built, 28
    German, 19
    Roman, 19
Viking age, 29
Sicily, 36
Siculus, Diodorus, 36
Sinclair, Henry, earl of Orkney, 32
Sir Orfeo, 100
Siricius, Pope, 14
Skekla, 120
Snorri Sturluson, 17, 48
Solway Firth, 13, 14
South Ronaldsay, 25
Spain, 22
Sutherland, 4, 63
Swedish, 62
Sykes, Brian, 53
syntax, 75

Tacitus, 17–18, 39–40
Tehran, 64
Thames, river, 20
Theodosius, emperor, 38, 40
Thule, 39
tin trade, 37
Torshavn, 6
Tyne, river, 20

Unst, 25, 52

Valens, emperor, 21
Valentinus, 45
Vandals, 22
Vikings, 25, 29, 88–9
  Danish, 54
  Norwegian, 54
Visigoths, 21
vocabulary, 76
Vortigern, 43, 44–5

Welsh, 14, 16, 25, 90
Western Isles, 7, 64, 91
Whithorn, 14
Wight, Isle of, 42, 45
Wigtownshire, 14
William Peace & Son publishers,
  105

Yaltmol, 60
Yell, 14
Yiddish, 87